On the cover: The neck shackle pictured was a common form of restraint during the first century. It was most often used when transporting prisoners from a conquered city or town, through open country, and to the captors' city.

The average person in the first century frequently saw . . . prisoners of war being marched through the streets on their way to becoming slaves. . . . Paul pictures the believer as one who has been set free by Christ (Gal. 5:1). Many of his references to spiritual freedom have their foundations in slavery because Christians have been bought with a price (1 Cor. 6:20; 7:23). Some members of the early congregations were slaves (1 Cor. 7:21) who would have clearly understood the concept of redemption.

William L. Coleman, *Today's Handbook of Bible Times and Customs*

Galatians
LETTER OF LIBERATION

BIBLE STUDY GUIDE

From the Bible-teaching ministry of

Charles R. Swindoll

INSIGHT FOR LIVING

Charles R. Swindoll is a graduate of Dallas Theological Seminary and has served in pastorates for more than twenty-four years, including churches in Texas, New England, and California. Since 1971 he has served as senior pastor of the First Evangelical Free Church of Fullerton, California. Chuck's radio program, "Insight for Living," began in 1979. In addition to his church and radio ministries, Chuck has written twenty-three books and numerous booklets on a variety of subjects.

Based on the outlines of Chuck's sermons, the study guide text is coauthored by Bill Watkins, a graduate of California State University at Fresno and Dallas Theological Seminary. The Living Insights are written by Bill Butterworth, a graduate of Florida Bible College, Dallas Theological Seminary, and Florida Atlantic University. Bill Butterworth is currently the director of counseling ministries at Insight for Living.

Editor in Chief:	Cynthia Swindoll
Coauthor of Text:	Bill Watkins
Author of Living Insights:	Bill Butterworth
Editorial Assistant:	Karene Wells
Copy Manager:	Jac La Tour
Senior Copy Editor:	Jane Gillis
Copy Editor:	Delia Mason
Director, Communications Division:	Carla Beck
Project Manager:	Nina Paris
Art Director:	Lonny Matsuda
Production Artist:	Donna Mayo
Typographer:	Bob Haskins
Calligrapher:	David Acquistapace
Cover Photograph:	G. Robert Nease
Print Production Manager:	Deedee Snyder
Printer:	Frye and Smith

ISBN 084-9982-944

Ordering Information

An album that contains twenty messages on ten cassettes and corresponds to this study guide may be purchased through Insight for Living, Post Office Box 4444, Fullerton, California 92634. For ordering information and a current catalog, please write our office or call (714) 870-9161.

Canadian residents may obtain a catalog and ordering information through Insight for Living Ministries, Post Office Box 2510, Vancouver, British Columbia, Canada V6B 3W7, (604) 272-5811. Australian residents should direct their correspondence to Insight for Living Ministries, General Post Office Box 2823 EE, Melbourne, Victoria 3001. Other overseas residents should direct their correspondence to our Fullerton office.

If you wish to order by Visa or MasterCard, you are welcome to use our toll-free number, (800) 772-8888, Monday through Friday, between the hours of 8:30 A.M. and 4:00 P.M., Pacific time. This number may be used anywhere in the continental United States except Alaska, California, and Hawaii. Orders from these areas can be made by calling our general office number, (714) 870-9161. Orders from Canada can be made by calling (604) 272-5811.

Table of Contents

Set Me Free! 1

Another Gospel Is Not *the* Gospel 10

A Radical Transformation 16

The Value of Acceptance and Affirmation 27

Confronting Hypocrisy 34

The Exchanged Life 40

Backsliding into Legalism 47

Delivered from a Curse 54

Three Men and a Promise 61

Preempting the Paidagogos 68

No Longer a Slave—a Son! 73

Solving the Pastor-People Conflict 80

To Those Who Want to Be under the Law 88

Freedom, Faith, Love, and Truth 95

Limiting Liberty with Love 103

Learning How to Walk 110

Gentle Restoration 116

The Law of the Harvest 123

A Bold, Blunt Reproof 131

A Branded Man 137

Books for Probing Further 145

Acknowledgments 148

Ordering Information/Order Forms 155

Galatians

I doubt if there is any greater joy on earth than the joy of being free. And the ecstasy is heightened if a person has once been in bondage, held captive by a power that seems impossible to overcome. Being liberated from such clutches brings pleasure beyond description.

Ask anyone who has been freed from prison. Or someone who was once held captive behind the Iron Curtain. Or worse, a victim of demonic oppression who is now free of that awful, frightening influence.

Equally delightful is the experience of being delivered from the paralyzing chains of legalism. There are few more dreadful dungeons! And yet many people today have relinquished their liberty and surrendered to the demands of the Law, selling themselves into the very slavery from which Christ came to deliver us. Worse yet, merchants of legalism abound—modern-day Judaizers who prey on unsuspecting Christians.

This letter sets us free. It is a bold statement of liberation, pointing us away from a "gospel" of works and toward the glorious grace Christ provides His own. May our Lord use these truths to free us from human bondage by the liberating power of His Spirit. As Jesus said, ". . . you shall know the truth, and the truth shall make you free" (John 8:32).

Chuck Swindoll

Putting Truth into Action

Knowledge apart from application falls short of God's desire for His children. Knowledge must result in change and growth. Consequently, we have constructed this Bible study guide with these purposes in mind: (1) to stimulate discovery, (2) to increase understanding, and (3) to encourage application.

At the end of each lesson is a section called **Living Insights.** There you'll be given assistance in further Bible study, and you'll be encouraged to contemplate and apply the things you've learned. This is the place where the lesson is fitted with shoe leather for your walk through the varied experiences of life.

In wrapping up some lessons, you'll find a unit called **Digging Deeper.** It will provide you with essential information and list helpful resource materials so that you can probe further into some of the issues raised in those studies.

It's our hope that you'll discover numerous ways to use this tool. Some useful avenues we suggest are personal meditation, joint discovery, and discussion with your spouse, family, work associates, friends, or neighbors. The study guide is also practical for Sunday school classes, Bible study groups, and, of course, as a study aid for the "Insight for Living" radio broadcast.

In order to derive the greatest benefit from this process, we suggest that you record your responses to the lessons in the space which has been provided for you. In view of the kinds of questions asked, your study guide may become a journal filled with your many discoveries and commitments. We anticipate that you will find yourself returning to it periodically for review and encouragement.

Bill Watkins
Coauthor of Text

Bill Butterworth
Author of Living Insights

Galatians
LETTER OF LIBERATION

Set Me Free!

Survey of Galatians

Few would deny that the most valued commodity in the world today is freedom. Some people seek release from political oppression; others strive to remove the chains of economic hardship. Teenagers fantasize about independence from their parents, employees dream about being their own bosses, and criminals long for their release from prison. Many still hope for liberty from racists, while others seek escape from overwhelming guilt. With so many of us looking for freedom, you would think we would have found it by now. But, for the most part, we haven't. As Eugene Peterson observes, "The actual lives that most people live are filled with impotence, boredom, obscurity, and hassle."[1] Sound familiar? Read on:

> Living in the land of the free has not made us free; we are a nation of addicts and complainers. Being provided with freedom of religion has not made us free; coercive cults and enslaving superstitions continue to proliferate. Assembling with people in church and listening to ringing proclamations of freedom—"He whom the Son sets free is free indeed!"—has not made us free. Our churches are attended regularly by the inhibited, the obsessive-compulsive, the fearfully defensive—enough of them to provide outside observers with a stereotype.[2]

Do these words strike a nerve in your soul? Are you bound by cords from which you long to escape? You *can* have freedom. You can experience it daily—wherever you live and whatever your circumstances. How? By applying the truths in the living letter of Galatians—an epistle inspired by God through the pen of His servant Paul. Come and join our pilgrimage from bondage to freedom in our study of Galatians. You have nothing to lose except the shackles that tie you down.

---

1. Eugene H. Peterson, *Traveling Light: Reflections on the Free Life* (Downers Grove, Ill.: InterVarsity Press, 1982), p. 9.

2. Peterson, *Traveling Light,* pp. 9–10.

I. Some Introductory Remarks on Galatians

The epistle of Galatians is the Magna Charta of Christian liberty. Like Abraham Lincoln's Emancipation Proclamation, Galatians shouts to believers in Christ, "You are free! You are free!" From what have we been freed? From trying to earn God's favor. How have we been freed? By grace alone . . . in Christ alone . . . through faith alone. For what have we been freed? For the joy of living an unshackled life based on grace, not the Law of Moses. Christians, however, frequently respond to the life of freedom in the same way that many slaves responded to their emancipation: they continue submitting to bondage rather than embarking on the free life made available to them. The Apostle Paul confronts this spiritual problem with a three-pronged attack.

A. A strong affirmation of liberty based on grace. Freedom from sin and the Law releases us from divine condemnation. God is no longer our adversary and judge but our protector and Father. He treats us as prodigal sons—forgiving our sins, canceling our debts, and celebrating our return home. In this kind of relationship, there's no room for lingering guilt. He has freed us from it so it won't stand in the way of an intimate relationship with Him. If you're a Christian still suffering from guilt, you need regular doses of Galatians. With consistent intake of its message, your soul will be cleansed and refreshed.

B. A bold assault on legalism based on works. Maintaining a list of dos and don'ts, rituals and traditions will not save us from sin and the deadening effects of guilt. Only trusting Christ as our personal Savior will bring the liberty we seek. Legalists don't like to hear this truth, but Galatians makes it clear that it is God's way of adopting us into His everlasting family.

C. A courageous encouragement for those surrounded by legalists. Again and again, Paul exhorts believers to stand up against the persuasive yet false arguments of legalists. He even uses himself as an example, telling how he opposed the hypocritical and legalistic actions of Cephas, also known as Peter (Gal. 2:11–21). Paul's example and message encourage us to fight for our freedom in Christ, refusing to bow down to those who seek to enslave us.

II. A Few Comments on the Letter's Value

Let's dig further into Galatians by examining four of its most valuable facets.

A. It warns against leaving the true gospel. After a brief greeting, Paul immediately jumps into the central issue without mincing words:

I am amazed that you are so quickly deserting Him
who called you by the grace of Christ, for a different
gospel; which is really not another [of the same kind
as the true gospel]; only there are some who are disturbing you, and want to distort the gospel of Christ.
But even though we, or an angel from heaven, should
preach to you a gospel contrary to that which we
have preached to you, let him be accursed. (1:6–8)

Christians who had been saved by faith *apart* from works were
now accepting a false gospel that taught salvation is by faith
plus works. Paul flatly states that this new gospel is not the
gospel at all. Indeed, it is a perversion of the truth, which is that
salvation is provided by God's merciful favor and can only be
received by faith in Jesus Christ. Add anything else—such as
church attendance, water baptism, or law-keeping—and the true
gospel is twisted into a false one. Paul says that people who
distort it are accursed, damned by God.

B. It upholds the significance of grace. Paul writes, " 'A
man is not justified by the works of the Law but through faith
in Christ Jesus . . . that we may be justified by faith in Christ, and
not by the works of the Law; since by the works of the Law shall
no flesh be justified. . . . I do not nullify the grace of God; for if
righteousness comes through the Law, then Christ died need-
lessly' " (2:16–21). Man cannot save himself. From the moment
of conception onward, he is alienated from God by sin, lacking
every ability to change his condition through his own efforts
(Job 14:1, 4; Pss. 51:1–5, 58:3; Rom. 5:12, 18–19; Eph. 2:3). By
choosing to trust in Christ, however, believing that His death
and resurrection provide the only basis for total forgiveness,
man can be justified before God. Justification is the sovereign
act of God whereby He declares the believing sinner righteous
while the sinner is still in a sinning state. This does not mean
that He looks on us as if we had never sinned. Rather, it means
that the Lord sets us free from the death penalty of sin and the
burden of guilt even while we are still disobeying Him. Now that's
a work of grace only God can perform!

C. It presents the true function of the Mosaic Law. Paul
says that the law revealed to Moses (Exod. 20–31) was "our tutor
to lead us to Christ, that we may be justified by faith" (Gal. 3:24).
Paidagōgos is the Greek word for "tutor," but it does not refer to
a teacher, as we might expect. Instead, it means "child-custodian,
child-attendant." Bible scholar James Montgomery Boice gives us
some background information to help us understand this word:

The pedagogue was a slave employed by wealthy Greeks or Romans to have responsibility for one of the children of the family. He had charge of the child from about the years six to sixteen and was responsible for watching over his behavior wherever he went and for conducting him to and from school. The pedagogue did not teach.... Paul's point is that this responsibility ceased when the child entered into the fullness of his position as a son, becoming an acknowledged adult by the formal rite of adoption by his father.[3]

In other words, the Law was our pedagogue; it was designed to protect us from overindulgence, expose our disobedience, and guide us to the gospel of grace. Once we accept Christ by faith, thereby becoming adopted children of God, we no longer need our tutor (vv. 25–26). Our heavenly Father takes us under His personal care, and the pedagogical slave retires to his quarters.

D. It provides needed balance between the abuse of liberty and the judgmental nature of legalism. Paul knew that the message of Christian freedom was often used as a license for sin. He combats this misunderstanding, pointing out that our liberty should be used to serve others lovingly, not to indulge the flesh (5:13–14). Paul also confronts the condemning finger of legalism with the compassionate hand of grace. He asks us to gently lift up and restore, not tear down and accuse, believers who have fallen into sin (5:26–6:1). When we really understand grace and make it a part of our lives, we use our freedom to obey the Lord and encourage His people. If you're a Christian, do you exercise your liberty this way? If not, pour yourself into the letter of Galatians, petitioning God to make its message motivate your heart to pursue a lifestyle that exudes grace.

III. An Overview of Its Content

Let's back away from some of the details of Galatians in order to view the big picture.

A. Its purpose. Galatians was written to defend the true gospel of grace against the counterfeit gospel of works. This purpose permeates every fiber of the letter.

B. Its characteristics. This epistle is vigorous, blunt, and brief. Paul let out all the stops in his fight for freedom, and history shows that he was successful. The principles declared and defended in this six-chapter letter successfully set Christianity apart from Judaism in the eyes of the world.

3. James Montgomery Boice, "Galatians," in *The Expositor's Bible Commentary,* 12 vols., ed. Frank E. Gaebelein (Grand Rapids, Mich.: Zondervan Publishing House, 1976), vol. 10, p. 467.

C. Its outline. Sandwiched between a ten-verse introduction and an eight-verse conclusion are the three major sections of Galatians. The first deals with the gospel's authenticity (1:11–2:21), the second with its superiority (3:1–4:31), and the third with its liberating lifestyle (5:1–6:10). A visual presentation of the epistle's structure is given in a chart found at the end of this lesson.

> ### Galatians as a Habit
> Before we wrap things up, let's make a personal commitment to read through Galatians every day for one month. This short letter doesn't take long to read—certainly each of us could find enough time. Would you begin doing this today? If you have several translations or paraphrases, you may want to alternate your reading between them. For example, one week you could use the New American Standard Bible, the next the New International Version, the following week the Living Bible, and the last week the New King James Version. This approach will help keep your reading fresh, opening up new vistas that will increase your understanding of Galatians.

IV. Some Principles to Apply

Galatians is doctrinally powerful and practically challenging. We dare not walk away from even a survey of this letter without considering how to carry out some of its truths.

A. No one is immune to the temptation to desert the gospel. Throughout church history, Christians have been lured away from the faith by propagators of counterfeit gospels. Today is no different. In the United States alone, more than twenty million people are members of non-Christian cults. Many, if not most, of these individuals were once members of mainline Protestant or Catholic churches.[4] You probably have family members or friends who at one time walked with Christ but now live according to an unbiblical standard. Don't look down on these people; instead, continually recall that as sinners, even saved ones, we are still prone to fall away from the truth. To combat this tendency, we must bathe ourselves in God's Word, allowing it to permeate every area of our lives.

B. Some things are worth a vigorous defense. The good news of salvation by faith alone is one of them. Like Paul, we need to uphold the true gospel, refuting objections to it and

---

4. See Walter Martin's *The Kingdom of the Cults,* rev. ed. (Minneapolis, Minn.: Bethany House Publishers, 1985), pp. 16, 390, 403–4.

exposing other alleged gospels as false. Our failure to do this in our own day has played a significant role in the explosive growth of counterfeit cults.[5] Are you involved in proclaiming and defending the gospel? As you gain a clear grasp of Galatians, you will be aided greatly in this task.

C. **We all begin at the same place, which puts us all on the same level.** We start out as rebels against God; then, through faith in His Son, we become coheirs of salvation and its many blessings. In Christ, "there is neither Jew nor Greek, there is neither slave nor free man, there is neither male nor female; for [we] are all one in Christ Jesus" (3:28). If you are not a Christian, this study in Galatians will make the plan of salvation clear. If you do know Christ as your Savior, guard against looking down on unbelievers or even fellow Christians; for you are still a sinner saved by God's grace apart from any work you could perform. You have nothing to boast about, but you do have a wonderful gift that God wants you to share in word and deed to all. If you haven't already done so, begin today to liberally offer His compassion to others through your own life.

 Living Insights

Study One

As we embark on our journey through this book of liberty, let's spend a few more moments developing an overview of the territory.

● As we suggested earlier, try reading through Galatians daily. While you read, use the chart on the next page to jot down anything in the book that stands out. To gain a broader understanding of the book, remember to read some different versions if they are available to you.

---

5. See Martin, *The Kingdom of the Cults,* pp. 390–91.

Observations: What does it say?

- Now that you've read through Galatians, can you think of a title for each chapter? Look for something that captures the key idea of the chapter. Be creative—many times it's the catchy titles that we remember!

Galatians	
Chapters	Titles
1	
2	
3	
4	
5	
6	

Continued on next page

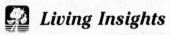 *Living Insights*

Read Galatians again, and keep the following questions in the back of your mind. Write your answers below when you have finished reading.

● How might the study of this book impact your life?

_____

_____

_____

_____

_____

● What verse or verses are personally significant to you? Why?

_____

_____

_____

_____

_____

● Do you struggle with grace versus the Law? If so, in what way?

_____

_____

_____

_____

_____

Galatians: "Set Me Free!"

Theme: Liberation through the gospel
Date: About A.D. 50 (Galatians may be Paul's first letter)
Key words: *law, faith, flesh*
Key verse: 5:1

Occasion: Galatians is an impassioned letter. Paul had heard that the Galatian Christians were falling away from the true gospel of grace and turning to a legalistic approach to salvation. He wished to turn them back to the freedom of salvation by faith alone. In doing so, he argued that not only is the sinner *saved* by grace, but the saved sinner also *lives* by grace. Grace is the way *to* life and the way of life.

	Introduction 1:1–10			Conclusion 6:11–18
	ISSUE OF TRUTH	NATURE OF SALVATION	PRINCIPLE OF HOLINESS	
	1:11 · Correction · Clarification · Confusion 2:21	3:1 · Bondage versus Freedom · Legalism versus Justification · Works versus Faith 4:31	5:1 · Don't be enslaved. · Serve through love. · Walk in the Spirit. · Bear one another's burdens. · Let us do good. 6:10	
	Personal Narrative	Doctrinal Argument	Practical Application	
	The Gospel Is Authentic (Source)	The Gospel Is Superior (Defense)	The Gospel Is Liberating (Impact)	
	The Authority of Paul's Apostleship	The Falsity of Legalism	The Power of God's Spirit	

© 1981 by Charles R. Swindoll

9

Another Gospel Is Not *the* Gospel

Galatians 1:1–10

As we learned in the first lesson, the gospel's central message is that Jesus Christ has graciously provided salvation from sin by dying in our place and rising from the grave. All we have to do to be saved is to trust in Christ and what He did on our behalf.

At the moment we accept Him and His work, we are delivered from the *penalty* of sin, which is everlasting separation from God. This aspect of salvation is known as justification (Rom. 3:21–30). Following our justification, we are gradually saved from the *power* of sin in our daily lives. In other words, we are sanctified, or made holy, as we spiritually grow up in God's family (1 Thess. 4:1–7). Our sanctification will be complete when we stand before the Lord, pure and immortal in body, soul, and spirit (1 Cor. 15:51–57, 2 Cor. 4:16, 1 Thess. 5:23, Jude 24). In this glorified state, we will be freed from the *presence* of sin, spending eternity with God in total bliss.

All three facets of salvation begin and reach fulfillment by God's grace— His undeserved favor poured out on sinful human beings. We cannot justify, sanctify, or glorify ourselves. Our salvation, from beginning to end, is a gift from God; we don't earn or achieve it in any way.

However, legalism says that we can't be saved without working for our deliverance in some way. Legalists claim that we must earn our salvation by adhering to a list of positives and negatives, dos and don'ts. But this so-called gospel is a fraud, as Paul so pointedly demonstrates in his letter to the Galatian Christians. Let's continue our study of this important book, focusing on its relevance to us today.

I. The Writer: Authority of Apostleship Asserted

Paul—the converted Pharisaic legalist once known as Saul of Tarsus (Acts 9:1–22, 22:3, 26:4–5)—is the human author of Galatians. He identifies himself in the opening sentence, as was the custom in his day (Gal. 1:1). He then goes on to state his role and express his greeting.

A. His role. Paul says in verse 1 that he is "an apostle (not sent from men, nor through the agency of man, but through Jesus Christ, and God the Father, who raised Him from the dead)." To become an apostle, a person had to have been (1) an eyewitness of Christ's ministry, including His resurrection and ascension, and (2) selected for the office by the risen Lord (Acts 1:21–26). Paul had fulfilled the second prerequisite, since he had encountered the resurrected Christ on his way to Damascus (9:3–6). The first requirement, however, was only partially met. Paul had seen Jesus after His resurrection but not before. Apparently, the legalists in Galatia were citing this fact in an attempt to undermine Paul's claim to be an apostle. But Paul points out that he had received his apostleship directly from God the Father and His Son, Jesus Christ. No mere human being had played even a minor role in his commission to this high office. Therefore, he, not the legalists, had the authority to speak for the Lord. This gives Paul the credentials he needs to perform radical spiritual surgery on the Galatian Christians and the legalists who were duping them.

B. His greeting. Paul's hello to the Galatian believers centers on the Christian gospel. He wishes them the grace and peace that comes from "God our Father, and the Lord Jesus Christ" (Gal. 1:3). Divine grace is the basis of the gospel, and peace between God and man is the result. Then Paul specifies that the price paid for the gospel was the life of Christ, "who gave Himself for our sins"; that the purpose of His death was our deliverance from "this present evil age"; and that this entire plan was "according to the will of our God and Father" (v. 4). In other words, the gospel is God's rescue operation, designed and implemented to liberate us from the oppression and penalty of sin. The cost of this mission was one life, that of God's own Son; the price was paid on a cross at Calvary. Because God originated this plan, set it in motion, paid its price, and carried it to fruition, He alone receives the glory for it (v. 5). We reap its benefits by placing our faith in Christ, but in no way do we receive any credit for the Lord's gracious provision.

A Crucial Clarification

Some people take verse 4 to an extreme, claiming that since we are saved from this world, we should not be concerned with what goes on around us. Because we are now in Christ, they argue, we are not of this world and one day will be taken out of it. Therefore, we have no responsibility to do anything for it. This thinking is surely false. Though eventually we will be removed from the world and taken up into heaven, in the meantime we are called by Christ to be light and salt in *this* world (Matt. 5:13–16). This means that we are obligated to the world in at least two ways: (1) to be beacons of the truth, drawing people toward us so they might see Christ in us, and (2) to be preserving agents, influencing society in a way that keeps the corrupting power of sin from finishing its destructive course. Never forget that the only everlasting things on earth are the Bible and people. Everything else will someday be destroyed and

---

replaced (2 Pet. 3:10–13). Therefore, we can best spend our brief lives here studying and obeying God's Word and evangelizing, discipling, and loving people. All other tasks are worthless in comparison.

II. The Message: Integrity of the Gospel Affirmed

Beginning in Galatians 1:6, Paul expresses astonishment and indignation. Undergirding his words is the expectation that Christians are to be thinkers with backbone who uphold the gospel message and do not dilute or taint it because of external pressures.

   A. Desertion for a "different" gospel. "I am amazed," Paul exclaims, "that you are so quickly deserting Him who called you by the grace of Christ, for a different gospel; which is really not another" (vv. 6–7a). The apostle was shocked that the Galatian believers were walking away from the true gospel, thereby deserting their Savior. Apparently, they had defected soon after their conversion to Christianity, at the time believers are most vulnerable to spiritual counterfeits. What were these Christians now accepting? A *heteros* gospel. This Greek term means "another of a different kind." The Galatian Christians were embracing a different gospel, and since there is only one true gospel, they were believing in a false one—one that is no gospel at all. It was a counterfeit gospel of works, claiming that faith in Christ plus performing certain acts would bring salvation. The difference between this gospel and the true one is all the difference in the world. The counterfeit leads to slavery and death; the true brings freedom and life. The Galatian Christians didn't see this difference. They thought they were accepting a complete view of God's salvation plan; in reality, they were transferring their allegiance to the oldest living deceiver—Satan.

   B. Disturbance within deluded souls. The Galatians' shift in loyalty caused them to lose internal peace (v. 7b). Doubt and agitation disturbed their souls, rooting out the inner assurance and harmony that accompanies the undistorted gospel.

   C. Reaction to false teachers. Perverting the gospel is a serious matter; it strikes at the very heart of the Christian faith. Realizing this, Paul responds with a curse aimed at anyone who would present a salvation plan that differs from the biblical one (vv. 8–9). False teachers, he says, are worthy of damnation—everlasting punishment in hell. He repeats this anathema twice, making it clear that people who twist the gospel deserve this awful final judgment. Why is this so? Because "both the glory of Jesus Christ and the salvation of men are at stake. If men can be saved by works, Christ has died in vain (Gal. 2:21); the cross is emptied of meaning. If men are taught a false gospel, they are being led from the one thing that can save them and are being turned to destruction (cf. Matt. 18:6)."[1]

III. The Conviction: Nonconformity of the Christian Upheld

Following his strong condemnation, Paul challenges his readers to find any hint of man-pleasing in his letter. He has not only blasted the legalists but rebuked those who were yielding to their heretical teaching. He could have been conciliatory, even compromising, but that would have made him as bad as they. So, choosing to remain "a bond-servant of Christ" rather than a pleaser of people (v. 10), Paul draws his literary guns and begins firing as the Holy Spirit leads. In doing so, he bares three principles we would do well to remember.

A. **Those who seek to please only God become invincible within.** When we serve the Lord diligently, our minds and hearts will not wander or become victimized by spiritual counterfeits. Our souls will become like steel, firmly cemented in the foundation of the Christian gospel. How solid is your foundation? Is it reinforced with a commitment of steel, bent on pleasing God only? Can it withstand the weight of counterfeits? Or does it crumble under pressure? If so, maybe you need to take an engineer's look at your life to determine whether pleasing God is truly an undergirding motivation (2 Cor. 5:9).

B. **Those who stop striving to please people are not intimidated by them.** There will always be those who try to lead us astray. But if our lives are centered on pleasing God rather than people, we will be able to stand strong when the lures come our way. Are you able to look intimidation in the face and stare it down? Or does it bring you to your knees, leading you to compromise your Christian faith? If so, you need to get your eyes back on God and surrender daily to the transforming work of His Spirit. This will enable you to overcome the temptation to place people above your commitment to the Lord.

C. **Those who are true servants of Christ think and act independently.** As Paul says, "If I were still trying to please men, I would not be a bond-servant of Christ" (Gal. 1:10b). We who are Christians should expose, confront, and refute any view that is contrary to the gospel of grace and the clear teaching of Scripture. Of course, doing so will often put us in a crowd of one. Are you willing to stand up and speak out for Christ? Are you in a situation that calls for independent thought and action? If so,

1. James Montgomery Boice, "Galatians," in *The Expositor's Bible Commentary*, 12 vols., ed. Frank E. Gaebelein (Grand Rapids, Mich.: Zondervan Publishing House, 1976), vol. 10, p. 429.

don't remain quiet. Speak the truth "with gentleness and reverence" (1 Pet. 3:15b), defending and doing what is right.[2]

 Living Insights

Study One ▬▬▬▬▬▬▬▬▬▬▬▬▬▬▬▬▬▬▬▬▬▬▬▬▬▬

The gospel ... its importance rings clear in this passage from Galatians. Paul attacks false teachers with the tenacity of a tiger! Why? Because understanding the unadulterated message of the gospel was paramount to the Galatians' growth ... and is to ours as well.

● What is the gospel of God's grace? Can you explain it? What Scriptures can you use to support the doctrine of salvation by grace through faith? In the chart below, fill in as many New Testament references concerning this doctrine as you can recall. Then consult a concordance and look up the words *grace, faith,* and *believe* in order to discover additional passages. Next to each reference, give a brief summary of its teaching.

The Gospel of Grace	
References	Summaries

2. You cannot defend Christianity if you're unclear about its basic doctrines or have a limited understanding of the attacks being made against it. The last section of this study guide, Books for Probing Further, lists several resources that will greatly aid you in these areas.

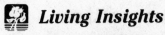 *Living Insights*

It's easy to pervert the gospel's truth. It's been done for centuries! In fact, we all probably know of people who distort God's grace by adding man's works to His message. Let's spend some time in prayer, asking God for wisdom in discerning what to read and who to listen to. Let's pray as well for our pastors and teachers, that they will strive to communicate God's one true gospel of grace.

A Radical Transformation
Galatians 1:11–24

The body of Christ in Galatia was suffering from cancer. The disease was wreaking havoc, tearing apart the church's unity and killing the testimony of her members. We have already identified the cancer—a counterfeit gospel of works. And we also learned that the disease took hold in Galatia through the infectious teaching of religious legalists known as Judaizers. They taught that salvation occurred when a sinner believed in Christ *and* kept the Law of Moses. Salvation by faith was insufficient; human achievement had to be added to bring deliverance from sin and death.

The Apostle Paul saw this cancerous growth and took strong measures to kill it. But the legalists didn't make it easy for him. They challenged him every step of the way, setting up barriers they thought were impregnable. Paul refused to back down. He pushed forward, scaling some walls and demolishing others.

Paul began by refuting their challenges to his apostolic authority and exposing their gospel of works as false (Gal. 1:1–9). Then he pressed further, knocking down their claim that he was not a true servant of God but a man-pleaser—a theological politician who cared more about human acceptance than divine favor (v. 10). Now, in the latter half of chapter 1, Paul deals with the most formidable argument yet: The gospel of grace is from man, not God.

I. The Origin of Paul's Message

The apostle refutes this argument, beginning with three denials and one affirmation. Let's look at the statements in the order he gives them.

A. Denials. First, Paul states that the gospel he preaches "is not according to man" (v. 11). No human being made it up. In fact, it's not the sort of belief people would invent. Man tends to flatter himself, making himself the searcher for God and the solver of evil. But Christianity turns this perspective on its head. It presents man running and hiding from God, committing crime after crime as the Lord pursues him with outstretched arms of mercy. If the Christian gospel, then, is not a human creation, could it have been communicated from one human to another until it finally came to Paul? The answer is no; Paul did not receive it through human tradition (v. 12a). "Well then," charge the Judaizers, "Paul must have been taught the gospel of faith by some person or institution." Once again, Paul responds in the negative (v. 12a).

B. Affirmation. From whom and how did Paul get his gospel message? "I received it," he answers, "through a revelation [from]

16

Jesus Christ" (v. 12b). The only human to touch the gospel before Paul was the God-man, Christ the Lord. Indeed, Jesus is the source, content, and goal of the Christian salvation message. Without Him, there is no revelation, no freedom, no hope—only fleeting pleasure and ultimate despair. The apostle claims that this Messiah has given him the message of liberation from sin by grace through faith. Paul is merely passing on what God the Son has told him to proclaim and defend.

A Twentieth-Century Update

Contrary to some people's assertions, God is not giving new revelations in our day. During the first century A.D., when the Scriptures were incomplete, God communicated His Word through prophets and apostles, giving the young Church needed direction and instruction. But with the completion of The Revelation to John, the last New Testament book to be written, the Bible was finished. So with the close of the first century came the end of divine written revelation. God still makes Himself known to individuals, and He continues to illumine our understanding and application of His Word. But He is not conveying new revelation to the Church—and hasn't for nineteen centuries.[1]

II. The Transformation of Paul

How can Paul demonstrate that his gospel is from God, not man? By appealing to his personal history: his life before, at, and after conversion.

A. Before conversion. Prior to accepting Christ, Paul was a persecutor of the Church and a Jew's Jew (vv. 13–14). He did everything in his power to destroy the Church:

> "I thought to myself that I had to do many things hostile to the name of Jesus of Nazareth. And this is just what I did in Jerusalem; not only did I lock up many of the saints in prisons, having received authority from the chief priests, but also when they were being put to death I cast my vote against them. And as I punished them often in all the synagogues, I tried to

---

1. Some excellent discussions of this issue can be found in *A General Introduction to the Bible,* rev. ed., by Norman L. Geisler and William E. Nix (Chicago, Ill.: Moody Press, 1986), chaps. 12–17; *The Old Testament Canon of the New Testament Church and Its Background in Early Judaism,* by Roger Beckwith (Grand Rapids, Mich.: William B. Eerdmans Publishing Co., 1986); and *Inspiration and Canonicity of the Bible,* by R. Laird Harris (Grand Rapids, Mich.: Zondervan Publishing House, 1957).

force them to blaspheme; and being furiously enraged at them, I kept pursuing them even to foreign cities." (Acts 26:9–11)

Paul's zealous commitment to a religion encrusted with human opinion, effort, and laws blinded him to the gospel's truth and the testimonies of Christians. All he could see was a people and a message that had to be annihilated because they contradicted what he firmly believed. Do you know people who, like Paul, are hateful toward you and Christianity because of their devotion to a non-Christian world view? Don't despair! If the Lord could save a militant unbeliever such as Paul, He can save anyone. Just continue to model and communicate the truth in a loving way, trusting God to take care of the rest.

B. At conversion.

"Now Saul [later known as Paul], still breathing threats and murder against the disciples of the Lord, went to the high priest, and asked for letters from him to the synagogues at Damascus, so that if he found any belonging to the Way, both men and women, he might bring them bound to Jerusalem. And it came about that as he journeyed, he was approaching Damascus, and suddenly a light from heaven flashed around him; and he fell to the ground, and heard a voice saying to him, 'Saul, Saul, why are you persecuting Me?' " (9:1–4)

At the height of Paul's antagonism to Christianity, Jesus broke into his life, softened his heart, and gave him the opportunity to repent. A few days later, Paul responded to this gracious offer, trusting in the same one he had adamantly persecuted only a short time before (vv. 17–19, 22:12–16). Reflecting on this event, Paul realized that it was not an accident or a spur-of-the-moment decision on God's part. The Lord had set him apart, even before his birth, for salvation through Christ (Gal. 1:15–16a). God is constantly engaged in our lives, not only during and after conversion, but before it as well (Jer. 1:4–5, Rom. 8:28–30, Eph. 1:3–5). He desires to transform our lives by revealing His Son to us so we might disclose Him to others. For Paul, the "others" were the Gentiles (Gal. 1:16)—all non-Jews, who were looked upon as filthy dogs by most Jews. Paul had been radically changed. This bigoted, bitter Jew had been turned by Christ into a lover of all peoples and a missionary of the gospel of grace. No mere human being could have brought about such an incredible transformation.

C. After conversion.
What did Paul do once he was saved? Did he enroll in seminary or teach Sunday school in a local church?

Not in the least! Paul says, "I did not immediately consult with flesh and blood, nor did I go up to Jerusalem to those who were apostles before me; but I went away to Arabia, and returned once more to Damascus. Then three years later I went up to Jerusalem" (vv. 16b–18a). We don't know exactly what Paul did during these three years, but we can be sure of one thing: it was a time of retraining and rethinking. After all, he had thought, felt, and behaved like a devout Jew all his life. Now he had to learn what Christianity was all about and change his life accordingly. Who taught him to do this? Since he had no human teachers, he must have had the divine instructor. Imagine taking a three-year course in Christian doctrine and life from the Messiah Himself!

Incubation Required

All too often, new believers are thrust into the limelight and given ministry responsibilities before they're ready to handle them. Paul's experience shows us that recently converted Christians need an environment conducive to spiritual growth. They need time to think about what has happened to them and to begin conforming their lives to the changes that have transpired within. If you know a new believer or are one yourself, take this spiritual incubation period seriously. Do what you can to encourage it. And don't rush this time along. God will end it when He sees fit.

Following his years in Arabia and Damascus, Paul journeyed to Jerusalem and spent fifteen days with Cephas—another name for Peter—in order to get acquainted with him (v. 18). During his brief visit, he didn't meet with any other apostle. The only other person he saw was "James, the Lord's brother" (v. 19). "Then," Paul adds, "I went into the regions of Syria and Cilicia. And I was still unknown by sight to the churches of Judea which were in Christ; but only, they kept hearing, 'He who once persecuted us is now preaching the faith which he once tried to destroy.' And they were glorifying God because of me" (vv. 21–24). The churches that once suffered under Paul's hatred were now strengthened by his ministry. And God received the praise because He made it all possible. The legalists stood refuted. The gospel of grace did come from the Lord, and it was adequately substantiated by Paul's testimony.

III. Our Response

Before we leave Paul's conversion story, let's draw out several truths we can apply.

A. When a person battles God, God always wins. We cannot beat Him. We will either yield to His love, thereby reaping the joys of heaven, or be conquered by His justice, thereby suffering the agonies of hell. The choice is ours, but the rules and the victory belong to Him. If we remember this, our lives will be touched with a deep sense of humility.

B. When God transforms a life, there is always a testimony. Our testimonies may not be as dramatic as Paul's, but they still stand as monuments of divine grace. Because of this, we need to share our conversion stories, lighting the path of faith for non-Christians as well as encouraging the spiritual sojourn of fellow believers. Here are some guidelines that can help you give your testimony in an effective way.

1. **Don't preach—just talk.** Let your story speak for itself.
2. **Don't generalize—be specific.** Name places, describe circumstances, identify feelings, share thoughts . . . communicate those elements that led up to, happened during, and followed your turn to Christ. You never know what God will use to soften stubborn wills and strengthen faint hearts.
3. **Don't be vague and mystical—be clear and simple.** Stay away from Christian lingo. Use language that anybody can understand, even those who have never heard about Christianity.
4. **Don't defend yourself—just declare your story.** People may try to explain away your conversion, or they may simply reject it. You are not responsible for their reaction. All God asks you to do is tell how He changed your life. The rest is up to Him.
5. **Keep your testimony brief.** Paul tells his story in twelve verses. You should be able to give yours in a few minutes.
6. **Follow a logical progression.** Start with your life before Christ, move to the moment of your conversion, then tell how Christ has changed your life.
7. **Glorify God, not yourself.** Although you are a primary actor in your conversion story, God is the star, the writer, and the director. Make this clear so that He gets the applause, not you.

A Practical Assignment

Share your testimony with a non-Christian sometime during the next week. God may use your story to begin yet another one that will eternally glorify Him.

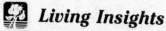

Living Insights

"When God transforms a life, there is always a testimony." Paul's life is no exception. We were briefly introduced to his story in Galatians, and we can pick up additional tidbits elsewhere in Scripture.

● Portions of Paul's life are described in Galatians 1:11–24; Acts 9:1–31, 26:4–23; and 2 Corinthians 11:22–33. Using the following chart, list under the appropriate headings what you observe in each passage. This will help you see in even greater detail Paul's radical transformation.

Before Christ	
Verses	Observations

Continued on next page

At Conversion	
Verses	Observations

After Christ	
Verses	Observations

Living Insights

"When a person battles God, God always wins." Because all of us who know Christ have thankfully lost our battle against Him, our personal testimonies are a great inspiration for others to lay down their weapons.

● Again, we encourage you to share your testimony with someone soon. In preparation, read over the tips given in the lesson. Using the three main headings of the previous chart, try to summarize each section of your life in writing. Aim for a testimony that could be given in about three minutes. That makes it brief and logical. And don't forget the other tips. Are you preaching? Are you specific, simple, and clear? Most of all, do you give God the glory for transforming your life?

My life before Christ: _____

_____

_____

_____

_____

My life at conversion: _____

_____

_____

_____

_____

My life after Christ: _____

_____

_____

_____

Continued on next page

Digging Deeper

Christ broke into Paul's life and turned him around 180 degrees. The Lord has been doing the same thing in the lives of others for centuries. Of course, not everyone is struck down by a blinding light as Paul was; nonetheless, people still come to the Savior, experience rebirth, and move forward to a new life of forgiveness and restoration. You may be interested in learning how other people have found freedom in Christ and how they worked out that freedom in their own lives. The following books are listed with this interest in mind. We think you'll discover more than information in their pages—you'll find a compassionate God who is actively at work bringing people like us to Himself to accomplish significant goals for His kingdom. Now that's encouraging!

- **God's Transforming Work in History**

Augustine, Saint. *Confessions.* Reprint. Translated by R. S. Pine-Coffin. New York, N.Y.: Penguin Books, 1979. Augustine was one of the greatest and most influential Christian thinkers who ever lived. He was born in A.D. 354, during the declining years of the Roman Empire, and until his conversion at age 32, he lived a life of wanton pleasure. In this book, he gives an account of his life before and after his new birth in Christ.

Bacon, Ernest W. *John Bunyan, Pilgrim and Dreamer.* Grand Rapids, Mich.: Baker Book House, 1983. The child of a mender and vendor of pots and pans, Bunyan went on to become a seasoned preacher and versatile writer in seventeenth-century Puritan England. Most of us know him best through his allegory of the Christian life, *Pilgrim's Progress.* Bacon tells Bunyan's life story in this sympathetic and historical book.

Carmen, Stephen L. *Quest.* With Bob Owen. Wheaton, Ill.: Tyndale House Publishers, 1986. In a day of scientific antagonism toward Christianity, Carmen, an aerospace engineer, shares how he turned from putting his faith in science to placing it in Christ.

Coe, Jolene and Greg. *The Mormon Experience.* Eugene, Oreg.: Harvest House Publishers, 1985. The fastest-growing cult today is Mormonism. Many are born into this counterfeit church, while many more are converted to it from Catholicism and Protestantism. This book is the story of one woman's journey from Mormonism to Christianity, from a childhood aspiration of being saved by works to an adulthood realization that salvation is by faith in Christ alone.

Colson, Charles W. *Born Again.* Old Tappan, N.J.: Chosen Books, 1976. Colson was one of President Nixon's most trusted and loyal workers, supporting the president regardless. Then came the political scandals that led Colson to a guilty plea and prison, and moved Nixon right out of the White House. But all was not lost. In fact, this was only the beginning of life for Colson. Here is his own account of the events that took him from Washington to Calvary, from political power to spiritual renewal.

Davis, Deborah (Linda Berg). *The Children of God: The Inside Story*. With Bill Davis. Grand Rapids, Mich.: Zondervan Publishing House, 1984. The tumultuous sixties saw the birth of the Children of God, a religious movement founded by David Berg. Berg's daughter, like other cult members, was dominated by her sinister father. In this book, she recounts her life in this bizarre movement and tells how she escaped its grip and ran into the arms of Christ.

Henry, Carl F. H. *Confessions of a Theologian: An Autobiography*. Waco, Tex.: Word Books, 1986. Perhaps no one has shaped the American evangelical movement more than Carl Henry. Among the many developments in which he played a major part are the founding of Fuller Theological Seminary and the magazine *Christianity Today*. This book tells the story from his birth in 1913 to his concerns for Evangelicalism in the eighties, nineties, and beyond.

Lewis, C. S. *Surprised by Joy: The Shape of My Early Life*. New York, N.Y.: Harcourt Brace Jovanovich, 1955. Many people have found Christ in reading Lewis's *Mere Christianity*. Others have been comforted by his books *The Problem of Pain* and *A Grief Observed*. Still others have delighted in his fictional works, such as *The Chronicles of Narnia* and his space trilogy. In *Surprised by Joy*, Lewis tells how the Savior brought him from atheism to Christianity, from fleeting happiness to everlasting joy.

Maharaj, Rabindranath R. *Death of a Guru*. With Dave Hunt. Philadelphia, Pa.: A. J. Holman Co., 1977. Rudyard Kipling wrote, "East is East, and West is West, and never the twain shall meet."[2] Today, with the pervasive influence of New Age Eastern beliefs, we can see that East is East and West is East—the two are now happily married. This book shows the bankruptcy of Eastern thought through the Christian eyes of a former Hindu guru. He explains how his search for meaning brought him to the feet of the way, the truth, and the life—Jesus Christ.

Murray, William J. *My Life without God*. Nashville, Tenn.: Thomas Nelson Publishers, 1982. Imagine growing up in the home of

2. *Bartlett's Familiar Quotations*, 14th ed., Emily Morison Beck, ed. (Boston, Mass.: Little, Brown and Co., 1968), p. 872.

Madalyn Murray O'Hair—one of the twentieth century's most outspoken atheists. Her son William Murray knows firsthand what it was like, and he reveals the hell he experienced on his sojourn to heaven's gate.

Pollock, John. *Wilberforce.* Belleville, Mich.: Lion Publishing Corp., 1977. John Pollock retells William Wilberforce's life in a moving, memorable way. Wilberforce was the reformer who campaigned relentlessly for the abolition of the slave trade in British territories. Just before his death, he witnessed Parliament's passage of the act that fulfilled his long-fought-for dream.

Schaeffer, Edith. *The Tapestry: The Life and Times of Francis and Edith Schaeffer.* Waco, Tex.: Word Books, 1981. In 1984, Francis Schaeffer went home to be with his Lord. He left behind a legacy of Christian compassion and excellence as a modern-day prophet and evangelist. His talented, supportive wife Edith displays the beautiful tapestry God weaved as He shaped their lives to fulfill His purpose.

Todd, John M. *Luther: A Life.* New York, N.Y.: Crossroad Publishing Co., 1982. This is a stirring account of the man who turned sixteenth-century Europe upside down by challenging the papacy with the Christian gospel. Luther was branded a heretic, excommunicated, and outlawed, but he never faltered because he found his fortress in God.

Vanauken, Sheldon. *A Severe Mercy.* New York, N.Y.: Bantam Books, 1977. This is a love story about a couple who married, met C. S. Lewis, and became believers, only to be shaken to the roots of their faith by a mysterious illness. You'll laugh and weep as you follow this elegantly written, powerful account of their dreams and fears, triumphs and defeats.

The Value of Acceptance and Affirmation

Galatians 2:1–10

Years ago, Anne Murray popularized a song that strikes a chord in us all.

> I cried a tear, you wiped it dry.
> I was confused, you cleared my mind.
> I sold my soul, you bought it back for me
>   and held me up and gave me dignity.
> Somehow you needed me.
> You gave me strength to stand alone again
>   to face the world out on my own again.
> You put me high upon a pedestal
>   so high that I can almost see eternity,
>   you needed me, you needed me;
>   and I can't believe it's you,
> I can't believe it's true.
> I needed you and you were there
>   and I'll never leave.
> Why should I leave I'd be a fool
>   'cause I've fin'lly found someone who really cares.[1]

Virtually all of us have had people help us put the pieces of our lives back together. They renewed us, strengthened us, cared for us, and believed in us. These encouragers may have been Christians who showed us what Christianity was all about by accepting us for who we were and affirming us for what we could become. They made us realize we were not only needed but wanted. How valuable their help! How precious our memory of them! How long has it been since you recalled what they did in your life? You'll get a chance to reminisce about them later in this lesson. And you'll be challenged to become an encourager yourself.

I. Reviewing Our Steps

Before pressing on to Galatians 2, let's capsulize chapter 1 in four statements by Paul.

A. I am "an apostle." Paul is not just anybody presenting the Christian gospel—he has been commissioned to his ministry by the resurrected Christ Himself, not by any mere mortal or local church (1:1, 15–24).

B. "I am amazed." Paul is shocked that the Galatian Christians are turning from the gospel that freed them from sin and the Law to a counterfeit gospel that reenslaves them (vv. 6–9).

---

1. "You Needed Me," by Randy Goodrum (Chappell and Co. and Ironside Music, 1975).

C. **"I received [the gospel] through a revelation."** Paul's message of grace came not from or through man but directly from Christ through a supernatural unveiling (vv. 11–12).

D. **"I am not lying."** The apostle reassures his readers that he is telling the truth (v. 20).

II. Visiting Jerusalem

Paul addresses a different charge in Galatians 2. In chapter 1, he shows his independence from the other apostles concerning his reception and understanding of the Christian gospel. This separation refutes the legalists' objection that his message is a distorted, human version of the true gospel. In chapter 2, however, Paul spends his energy spelling out his close relationship with the apostolic church leaders. He does this to answer the argument that the gospel he taught was not approved by these high officials. Paul explains that not only he but also his message was accepted and affirmed by the apostles, launching him into a ministry greater than he had before.

A. **Paul's companions.** Fourteen years after his first visit to Jerusalem to see Peter (1:18), Paul went back with Barnabas and Titus (2:1). The fourteen-year time period indicates how long Paul had been preaching the gospel of grace among Gentiles before returning to any of the other apostles. And on this visit, he didn't come alone. He brought Titus, a Gentile believer the legalists thought should be circumcised (vv. 3–4). Titus was a test case for the validity of the gospel of faith plus nothing. His conversion stood as evidence that one could be saved apart from the works required by the Mosaic Law. Paul's other companion, Barnabas, was a circumcised Jewish believer. His name means "Son of Encouragement" (Acts 4:36), and he filled it to the letter, especially in Paul's life. After Paul found salvation, Barnabas vouched for him to the apostles who had first rejected him out of fear (9:26–27). Later, Barnabas was sent by the church leaders in Jerusalem to investigate what they had heard about Gentiles accepting the Christian faith in Antioch (11:19–22). Barnabas confirmed the reports, and he spent time encouraging the new converts and their ministers. Realizing that Paul could help him tremendously, Barnabas left Antioch in search of him. The two men returned to Antioch and worked for a year together, grounding spiritually young Christians in their faith (vv. 23–26). Barnabas repeatedly demonstrated that he believed in Paul. No wonder Paul brought him along on his return visit to Jerusalem.

B. **Paul's message.** The apostle emphasizes that his prolonged absence from Jerusalem ended because he had received a revelation (Gal. 2:2a). We don't know how this revelation came to him, but we can infer its content from Paul's account. He was told to go to Jerusalem to meet privately with some of the most respected leaders of the church. The purpose of this meeting was not to verify the truth of his gospel message, for Christ had already done so in previous revelations. Rather, Paul journeyed to Jerusalem to get the highest stamp of human approval for his gospel of grace and ministry to the Gentiles (vv. 2a, 6–9). Why? So the church could be unified and his critics defanged. After all, if the apostles gave Paul their support, no one could challenge him by claiming they also had the backing of the church's leadership.

C. Paul's critics. Wherever Paul went, the legalists dogged his steps. For instance, they caused dissension during his ministry in Antioch, teaching the Christians that they could not be saved unless they were circumcised according to the Mosaic Law (Acts 15:1–2). These legalists were not simply deluded Christians. Paul calls them "false brethren"—bogus believers "who had sneaked in to spy out our liberty which we have in Christ Jesus, in order to bring us into bondage" (Gal. 2:4). How did Paul, his companions, and the other apostles respond to them? Paul tells us in no uncertain terms: "We didn't give them the time of day—we were determined to preserve the truth of the gospel for you" (v. 5; compare Acts 15:4–29).[2] Nothing was added to or subtracted from the gospel of salvation by grace alone through faith alone. The church leaders stood as one and dashed the legalists' hopes of dividing and conquering the human hierarchy of Christ's Church.

D. Paul's endorsement. The men who upheld Paul, his ministry, and his message were James, Peter, and John—all apostles Paul calls men "of reputation," "of high reputation," and "who were reputed to be pillars [of the church]" (Gal. 2:2, 6, 9). These men had tremendous authority and influence. In fact, between them, they wrote seven of the New Testament books. If we include Paul's writings, we have the human authors of twenty of the New Testament's twenty-seven books. This conference was a summit meeting of the highest order. And these great leaders gave their total support to Paul and Barnabas, offering them "the right hand of fellowship, that [they] might go to the Gentiles" as they had done in the past (v. 9). The only request these men added was that Paul and his co-workers "remember the poor," a request Paul was eager to keep (v. 10). Let's zoom in on the threefold endorsement given to Paul and explore what it says to us today.

---

2. Translation by Eugene H. Peterson, *Traveling Light: Reflections on the Free Life* (Downers Grove, Ill.: InterVarsity Press, 1982), p. 59.

1. **They saw Paul's distinctive contribution.** The apostolic leaders realized that Paul "had been entrusted with the gospel to the uncircumcised, just as Peter had been to the circumcised" (v. 7). God had gifted Paul to meet the needs of a certain group of people, and Paul used his gifts to do what God wanted him to accomplish. The Lord does the same today. Each of us has been given varied abilities and desires to serve different kinds of people. We need to discover what our gifts are and cultivate and use them to honor God.[3] Likewise, we should help less mature believers find and develop their unique talents and drives rather than try to shape them into preset, ministry-squelching molds.

2. **They accepted Paul as much as they did Peter.** The church leaders saw that although Peter and Paul had diverse ministries, their energy was from the same source—God (v. 8). Therefore, they approved and supported each man and his work. We, too, need to affirm others whose lives bear the handprint of God. All Christians, especially new ones, need to be accepted for who they are and what they can become in Christ. This applies equally to children. Parents have the responsibility to encourage the development of their offspring and help them discover their own talents.[4]

3. **They recognized the grace given to Paul and encouraged him to press on.** Seeing that Paul had been given the style, gifts, passion, and direction to minister to the Gentiles, the apostles urged him to keep at his divinely appointed task (v. 9). How little it seems we Christians encourage one another to keep on keeping on, to continue doing what God has called us to do. We desperately need to hear and give words of affirmation and edification so the Lord's work will flourish, even in spite of opposition.

III. Encouraging an Encourager

Who has strengthened you in your walk with God? Who has accepted and affirmed you when no one else came to your side? Perhaps you can recall only one person who really upheld you in confusing or hard times. Or maybe several people come to mind. Regardless of

---

3. For some welcome help in this area, see the study guide *Spiritual Gifts,* coauthored by Ken Gire, Jr., from the Bible-teaching ministry of Charles R. Swindoll (Fullerton, Calif.: Insight for Living, 1986).

4. Some helpful resources on childrearing and spiritual development are: *You and Your Child,* by Charles R. Swindoll (Nashville, Tenn.: Thomas Nelson Publishers, 1977); *Teaching Your Child about God,* by Wes Haystead (Ventura, Calif.: Regal Books, 1974); *Growing Up in God's Family,* ed. Bill Watkins, from the Bible-teaching ministry of Charles R. Swindoll (Fullerton, Calif.: Insight for Living, 1986); and *In Pursuit of Maturity,* by J. Oswald Sanders (Grand Rapids, Mich.: Zondervan Publishing House, 1986).

the number, remember those who have encouraged you and thank God for them. If you can, voice your appreciation to them, encouraging them to press on in the tasks God has designed especially for them. In this way, you will give back some of what they have lovingly given to you.

 Living Insights

Study One ▬▬▬▬▬▬▬▬▬▬▬▬▬▬▬▬▬▬▬▬▬▬▬▬▬▬▬▬▬▬▬

A frequently used aid in understanding a passage of Scripture is to discover the meaning of the verbs it contains. The verbs in this passage have a distinct heartbeat. Let's check it out.

● Slowly read through Galatians 2:1–10 and circle fifteen of the verbs you find. Write them in the spaces below. Briefly define each word. Feel free to consult a dictionary.[5] Finally, try to explain in a few words why that verb is significant to the passage.

Galatians 2:1–10

Verse: _____ Verb: _____

Definition: _____

Significance: _____

_____

Verse: _____ Verb: _____

Definition: _____

Significance: _____

_____

Verse: _____ Verb: _____

Definition: _____

Significance: _____

_____

---

5. Some useful Bible dictionaries are: *Unger's Bible Dictionary,* by Merrill F. Unger (Chicago, Ill.: Moody Press, 1966); *Nelson's Illustrated Bible Dictionary* (Nashville, Tenn.: Thomas Nelson Publishers, 1986); and *The Zondervan Pictorial Bible Dictionary* (Grand Rapids, Mich.: Zondervan Publishing House, 1967).

Verse: _____ Verb: _____

Definition: _____

Significance: _____

_____

Verse: _____ Verb: _____

Definition: _____

Significance: _____

_____

Verse: _____ Verb: _____

Definition: _____

Significance: _____

_____

Verse: _____ Verb: _____

Definition: _____

Significance: _____

_____

Verse: _____ Verb: _____

Definition: _____

Significance: _____

_____

Verse: _____ Verb: _____

Definition: _____

Significance: _____

_____

Verse: _____ Verb: _____

Definition: _____

Significance: _____

_____

Verse: _____ Verb: _____

Definition: _____

Significance: _____

_____

Verse: _____ Verb: _____

Definition: _____

Significance: _____

_____

Verse: _____ Verb: _____

Definition: _____

Significance: _____

_____

Verse: _____ Verb: _____

Definition: _____

Significance: _____

_____

Verse: _____ Verb: _____

Definition: _____

Significance: _____

_____

 Living Insights

Study Two ▬▬▬▬▬▬▬▬▬▬▬▬▬▬▬▬▬▬▬▬▬▬▬▬▬▬▬

Have you adequately conveyed your appreciation to a person who has encouraged and believed in you? Perhaps it's time to do that right now.

• Write a letter of appreciation to that special friend. Get beyond the cold facts. Tell how deeply you feel and explain your circumstances at that time in your life. Conclude by sharing what God is doing in your life now.

Confronting Hypocrisy

Galatians 2:11–16, Acts 14:24–15:11

Live and let live . . . do your own thing . . . if it feels good, do it . . . you mind your business and I'll mind mine. These popular expressions reveal our culture's pervasive perspective: we are accountable to no one but ourselves. Like bubbles, we go our own ways with no regard to the paths taken by others. And when we bump into one another on occasion, we rarely allow anyone to penetrate the surface of our lives.

Has this viewpoint infiltrated the Church? You bet it has! We hardly ever treat ourselves as members of Christ's united family. The closeness, care, forgiveness, and accountability that marks a loving family are all but invisible in our local churches. Instead, most Christians lead lives centered on benefiting themselves, often at the expense of others. While the harm is usually not intentional, it is just as damaging as if it were.

Is this biblical? Are we to live independently, minding our own business even when we see someone scandalize the Body of Christ? Don't you believe it! God's Word exposes this two-faced lifestyle as hypocrisy, telling us to face it squarely and openly so we can build up one another in Christian maturity. The Scriptures we'll examine bear out this truth through a confrontation between two apostles—Paul and Peter.

I. Why Is This Incident Recorded in Galatians?

The conflict we will focus on is described in Galatians 2:11–16:

> But when Cephas came to Antioch, I opposed him to his face, because he stood condemned. For prior to the coming of certain men from James, he used to eat with the Gentiles; but when they came, he began to withdraw and hold himself aloof, fearing the party of the circumcision. And the rest of the Jews joined him in hypocrisy, with the result that even Barnabas was carried away by their hypocrisy. But when I saw that they were not straightforward about the truth of the gospel, I said to Cephas in the presence of all, "If you, being a Jew, live like the Gentiles and not like the Jews, how is it that you compel the Gentiles to live like Jews? We are Jews by nature, and not sinners from among the Gentiles; nevertheless knowing that a man is not justified by the works of the Law but through faith in Christ Jesus, even we have believed in Christ Jesus, that we may be justified by faith in Christ, and not by the works of the Law; since by the works of the Law shall no flesh be justified."

Why does Paul present this clash of opinions to the Galatian Christians? At least two reasons are evident.

34

A. Historical. From the letter's historical context, we can gather that Paul included this incident to further refute the legalists' charge that he had no apostolic authority. As James Boice points out, "the Galatians were to realize that Paul was not a self-appointed apostle, nor even a worker appointed and approved by the Twelve. He was rather a full apostle in his own right, who could therefore speak with full authority even, if necessary, in opposition to another apostle."[1]

B. Practical. This confrontation also illustrates that Christians are accountable to one another. We are not islands unto ourselves, but equal members of God's forever family, responsible to one another and our Lord to grow up in godliness. When any of us departs from this obligation, intentionally or not, we should be confronted and brought back with Christian love and compassion. No matter how gifted, important, or popular, none of us are exempt from spiritual accountability.

II. What Occurred and When?

Let's try to understand what happened before we draw out the ramifications.

A. The context. Luke does not mention this encounter between Peter and Paul in the Acts of the Apostles. Perhaps he was unaware of their clash, or maybe he felt the matter was too private to include. Whatever the case, the Holy Spirit thought it best to leave it out of Luke's historical record. Although this omission makes it difficult to determine the exact time of the confrontation, it probably happened in Antioch after Paul's first missionary journey (Acts 14:24–28, Gal. 2:11). This would place Paul's rebuke of Peter prior to the first church council meeting in Jerusalem, the one that officially and publicly recognized that salvation is received by faith apart from the regulations of the Law (Acts 15:1–29).

B. The event. While in Antioch, Peter—referred to as Cephas in the text—"used to [regularly] eat with the Gentiles" (Gal. 2:12a). This practice was taboo in Jewish circles, but Peter had learned in a revelation that God viewed it differently. In this vision, the Lord encouraged Peter to break with his Jewish heritage—to eat food and be with people that had been declared unclean (Acts 10:1–11:18). Peter obeyed God. Yet when some influential Jews arrived in Antioch from Jerusalem claiming to be representatives of James, Peter "began to withdraw and hold himself aloof" from the Gentile believers (Gal. 2:12). Why did he do this? Because he feared the legalists—"the party of the circumcision"

---

1. James Montgomery Boice, "Galatians," in *The Expositor's Bible Commentary*, 12 vols., ed. Frank E. Gaebelein (Grand Rapids, Mich.: Zondervan Publishing House, 1976), vol. 10, p. 446.

(v. 12b). Bowing to peer pressure, Peter was denying the very principles he held to be true. And, no doubt, he also refused to join the Gentile Christians in celebrating the Lord's Supper—the meal at which they remembered the death of their Lord for their sins.[2] Peter's actions caused a split between the Jewish and Gentile believers: "And the rest of the Jews joined him in hypocrisy, with the result that even Barnabas was carried away by their hypocrisy" (v. 13). The Greek term for *hypocrisy* means "play-acting, pretending, wearing a disguise."[3] Peter and those who followed his example knew they were wrong. But they pretended they were right, putting on self-righteous masks that Paul exposed and ripped away when he saw "they were not straightforward about the truth of the gospel" (v. 14a). Paul confronted Peter in front of everyone, recounting what Peter knew was true; namely, that neither Jew nor Gentile is saved "by the works of the Law but through faith in Christ Jesus, . . . since by the works of the Law shall no flesh be justified" (v. 16).

C. The reason. Why did Paul rebuke Peter? The reason is simple: Peter's actions were wrong, and they had a harmful effect on the lives of others. Peter betrayed the heart of the gospel by adding obedience to the Law as a condition of salvation. He did this not because he accepted justification by works as true, but because he succumbed to peer pressure. Paul realized he could not allow this two-facedness to go unchallenged. He also knew that the gravity of Peter's public hypocrisy demanded a public rebuke. Indeed, Paul's response was well within the boundaries of scriptural principles. Disobedience to the truth must be exposed (Eph. 5:11). And public rebuke should occur when a charge against a church leader is substantiated by at least two witnesses (1 Tim. 5:19–20). Furthermore, the confrontation should be public "so that the rest [of the people] also may be fearful of sinning" (v. 20b). Paul had a church full of witnesses, some of whom were participants in Peter's sin. Therefore, he had the proper validation and reason to oppose Peter in front of the congregation.

A Point to Ponder

When essential truths are at stake, they should be defended, even at the risk of losing close friends, financial security, or popular support. People, possessions, power,

---

2. See Alan Cole's commentary, "The Epistle of Paul to the Galatians," in *The Tyndale New Testament Commentaries* (Grand Rapids, Mich.: William B. Eerdmans Publishing Co., 1965), p. 74.

3. See the entry "Lie, Hypocrite" by Walther Günther in *The New International Dictionary of New Testament Theology* (Grand Rapids, Mich.: Zondervan Publishing House, 1976), vol. 2, pp. 467–70.

and prestige are not as important as Christ. If we don't believe this is true and act accordingly, we are in danger of accommodating false beliefs and immoral lifestyles, which God will not tolerate for long (Heb. 2:1–4, 10:26–38).[4]

D. The outcome. How did Peter respond to Paul's rebuke? Galatians 2 doesn't tell us, but church history shows that Peter once again became a stalwart of the faith (compare 1 and 2 Peter). If his run-in with Paul occurred prior to the first church council in Jerusalem, we can see in Acts 15:1–11 that Peter was led to stand up for the Christian gospel in the face of strong opposition from Judaizing legalists.

III. How Does This Apply to Us?

This study contains a number of applications, but let's look at four of the most important.

A. Christians are accountable to one another. We do not have the right to live as we please and expect everyone else to look the other way. God's standard of living applies to us all, and we are to help one another maintain it—even if it involves private or public confrontation. But the rebukes we give should be offered with genuine love and concern for those who falter (Ps. 141:5, Prov. 27:6). The Body of Christ has no room for disrespect or revenge.

B. Christians do impact one another. Whether or not people actually model their lives after ours, we are influencing them for better or worse. As Christians, we represent Christ to a watching world, so let's conduct our lives in a way that honors Him.

C. Christians should be committed to the truth. God is truth, and His revelations in creation and Scripture accurately convey truth (Pss. 19:1, 33:4, 119:160; Prov. 30:5–6; John 17:17; Acts 14:17; Rom. 1:18–20). Therefore, we deny Him and violate His character when we compromise the truth. Of all people, we who are believers should be known for our unwavering commitment to all that is true and right.

D. Christians should uphold a holy standard of living. The Apostle Peter says it best: "As obedient children, do not be conformed to the former lusts which were yours in your ignorance, but like the Holy One who called you, be holy yourselves also in all your behavior; because it is written, 'You shall be holy, for I am holy'" (1 Pet. 1:14–16).

---

4. For some excellent explanations of the essentials of Christianity, see *Know What You Believe,* by Paul E. Little (Wheaton, Ill.: Victor Books, 1970); and *Lectures in Systematic Theology,* by Henry C. Thiessen, rev. Vernon D. Doerksen (Grand Rapids, Mich.: William B. Eerdmans Publishing Co., 1979).

Living Insights

The Scripture passages we've studied sound like they came right off the front page of the *Antioch Times-Herald.* Peter and Paul create quite a newsworthy story.

• As a reporter for your local newspaper, you've been assigned this story. Investigate it by asking who, what, where, when, why, and how. Be sure to check out these references—Galatians 2:11–16; Acts 14:24–28, 15:1–35. Based on the facts you gather, put your story together and give it a headline.

Who? _____

What? _____

Where? _____

When? _____

Why? _____

How? _____

Antioch Times-Herald

Date: _____ Antioch, Syria _____ Volume: _____

_____

(Headline)

_____

_____

_____

_____

_____

_____

_____

_____

_____

_____

_____

_____

_____

_____

_____

_____

🌳 *Living Insights*

We are not islands; we belong to one another as members of God's family. Because of this, we have a responsibility to be accountable to God and fellow believers for our actions.

- This lesson concluded with four areas of practical application. Evaluate how you're doing in these areas and check (√) the appropriate response.

  Accountability to Christians: ☐ Doing Well ☐ OK ☐ Needs Work

  Impact on others: ☐ Doing Well ☐ OK ☐ Needs Work

  Commitment to truth: ☐ Doing Well ☐ OK ☐ Needs Work

  Standard of living: ☐ Doing Well ☐ OK ☐ Needs Work

- Which area or areas need work? How can you improve? List three things you can do this week; ask God for His help.

  1. _____

  2. _____

  3. _____

The Exchanged Life

Galatians 2:17–21, Isaiah 40:28–31

What a day. The children fussed and fought...the washing machine went berserk...your husband called at 4:30 to say he is bringing a client home for dinner. And this has been one of your better days! You sink down in a kitchen chair, too tired even to cry. Where will you get the strength to go on?

Or maybe you've come to the end of another high-pressure, sixty-hour workweek. Your boss just left the office, giving you a pile of work that can't wait until Monday. All you want to do is go home and crawl into bed, but you're too exhausted to even walk out to your car. You close your office door and slump down at your desk. With tears in your eyes, you wonder if constant fatigue and overload is the burden you will always carry.

Is there another way to live? Can you find relief even at the height of life's many demands? The answer is in the *exchanged life*—an idea that's expressed physically in Isaiah and spiritually in Galatians. Let's turn to Isaiah first, because it provides the basis for our comprehension of the Galatians passage.

I. Insights from Isaiah

Most of Isaiah 40 speaks about God's incomparable greatness. He is infinitely majestic—sovereign over all, knowing all things, and controlling nature by His incredible power. Because He is eternal and unlimited in strength, He "does not become weary or tired" (v. 28). Nor does He keep His abundant energy to Himself: "He gives strength to the weary, / And to him who lacks might He increases power" (v. 29). How does He do this? Must we meet any conditions before we can draw upon His power? Verse 31 gives us the answers.

A. What we must do. God gives His strength to "those who wait for the Lord" (v. 31a). What is involved in waiting for Him? The Hebrew term translated *wait* means "to twist, to stretch." In its noun form, it refers to a measuring line or a rope. When these meanings are combined, the term conveys the picture of a strand of hemp that alone is fragile; but when twisted around another strand, which in turn is twisted around another and another, it becomes a strong rope. We must stop trying to make it on our own and, instead, wrap our trust around God—the source of eternal power.

B. What God will do. When we finally turn to the Lord, relying on Him to give us relief, we "will gain new strength" (v. 31a). Indeed, the lift will be so great that we'll soar "like eagles,...run and not get tired,...walk and not become weary" (v. 31b). That's

40

the kind of energy we need, and it's available to us when we trade our weakness and weariness for God's strength and energy.[1]

II. Principles from Paul

The spiritual counterpart of Isaiah 40:28–31 is Galatians 2:17–21. Although the key principle of both passages is similar, their contexts are not. Paul does not talk about the greatness of God, but he does defend his apostleship and the Christian gospel against the charges of the legalistic Judaizers. These people were Jews parading as Christians, teaching that faith in Christ was insufficient for salvation. They argued that to be justified, one must believe in Christ *and* obey the Mosaic Law. Paul clearly sees that their gospel of works not only contradicts the Old Testament's teaching that salvation is by faith alone (Gal. 3:6–9; compare Rom. 4:1–22, Heb. 11)[2] but denies the relevance of Christ's death (Gal. 2:21). Furthermore, a salvation even partially based on human deeds leads to uncertainty regarding one's destiny. How could we ever know when enough good works have been performed to warrant a place in heaven? Obviously, since we can't know for sure, we would have to work overtime to gain any sense of assurance about the future. This lifestyle is bound to produce physical and psychological fatigue as well as spiritual unrest. Paul rightly condemns this perverted gospel, contending that faith, not human conduct, is the only means for coming into a right relationship with God. But Paul's view of salvation leaves him open to another of the Judaizers' objections—that justification by faith is a license for immorality (v. 17). James Boice paraphrases their argument:

> "Your doctrine of justification by faith is dangerous, for by eliminating the law you also eliminate a man's sense of moral responsibility. If a person can be accounted righteous simply by believing that Christ died for him, why then should he bother to keep the law or, for that matter, why should he bother to live by any standard of morality? There is no need to be good. The result of your doctrine is that men will believe in Christ but thereafter do as they desire."[3]

Let's see how Paul responds to the Judaizers in Galatians 2:17b–21.

---

1. See *Interpreting Isaiah: The Suffering and Glory of the Messiah,* by Herbert M. Wolf (Grand Rapids, Mich.: Zondervan Publishing House, 1985), p. 187.

2. A careful, insightful study of the Old Testament's doctrine of salvation is provided by John S. Feinberg in his essay "Salvation in the Old Testament" in *Tradition and Testament: Essays in Honor of Charles Lee Feinberg,* ed. John S. Feinberg and Paul D. Feinberg (Chicago, Ill.: Moody Press, 1981), pp. 39–77.

3. James Montgomery Boice, "Galatians," in *The Expositor's Bible Commentary,* 12 vols., ed. Frank E. Gaebelein (Grand Rapids, Mich.: Zondervan Publishing House, 1976), vol. 10, p. 450.

A. Justification before God. Paul denies that his gospel message leads one to an ungodly lifestyle (v. 17b). It marks, in fact, the beginning of a radically changed life—a new creation intent on serving God, not on rebelling against Him (2 Cor. 5:14–19). Of course, Christians still sin, but neither Jesus nor the gospel of grace is the cause—it comes from our sinful nature (James 1:13–17).

B. Death to the Law. Believers who insist on keeping the Law as a requirement for their salvation prove that they are sinners (Gal. 2:18). Why? Because they cannot keep all the Law's demands. Consequently, they stand condemned to death by the very standard they believe gives them life (v. 19a; compare 3:10, 21; Rom. 3:19–20). Therefore, the Law shuts the door to all hope that salvation can be earned. However, when doing so, it opens the window to discovering new life in God through faith alone (Gal. 2:19).

C. Life in Christ. How can we receive this new life? Ironically, it comes when we die with Christ—when, by faith, we wrap ourselves around Him so completely that our sinful selves are crucified with Him and we are reborn with Christ living in us (v. 20). In this born-again state, we live the exchanged life on the spiritual level. We give ourselves to Christ and He gives Himself to us, empowering us with His infinite strength so we can live as He desires. Once we're justified by faith, we cannot help but live transformed lives—lives that display an increasing commitment to Christian beliefs and practices.[4]

Making the Abstract Concrete

If this idea is difficult for you to grasp, perhaps an illustration will help. Suppose you want to become a concert pianist, but you can't play a note of music. A virtuoso pianist comes to you and says, "I have the ability to join with you in such a way that I can play the piano through you, using your hands, feet, will, and mind. But I won't unless you believe I can and will do it. Will you trust me?" Delighted, you trustingly sit down at the piano and begin to play. Your fingers caress the keys, creating a brilliant blend of harmony and melody. Soon a crowd gathers, enjoying every note. When you stop, the audience applauds heartily. Instead of taking a bow for yourself, you explain that you were merely a trusting instrument of the real maestro.

---

4. A fascinating exploration of the changes that occur in our spirit, soul, and body at and after conversion is given by Winfried Corduan in *Handmaid to Theology: An Essay in Philosophical Prolegomena* (Grand Rapids, Mich.: Baker Book House, 1981), chap. 10.

Someone else performed through you; without help, you could not have played even a simple scale. Likewise, Christ is the master musician who wants to perform beautiful music through us, if we will only believe in Him and stop trying to play the instrument by ourselves.

III. Guidelines to Live By

Reflecting on what we've discovered in this lesson, let's concentrate on three truths that pertain to us all.

A. Our greatest need is to be accepted by God. We don't need a good reputation, a loving family, a caring church, or a sense of purpose as much as we need a right relationship with God. The Apostle Paul boldly expresses this reality:

> I count all things to be loss in view of the surpassing value of knowing Christ Jesus my Lord, for whom I have suffered the loss of all things, and count them but rubbish in order that I may gain Christ, and may be found in Him, not having a righteousness of my own derived from the Law, but that which is through faith in Christ, the righteousness which comes from God on the basis of faith, that I may know Him, and the power of His resurrection and the fellowship of His sufferings, being conformed to His death; in order that I may attain to the resurrection from the dead. (Phil. 3:8–11)

Have you been justified by faith?

B. Our only hope of peace with God is salvation through Christ. The Mosaic Law cannot save us. Nor can church membership. Living a good life or sacrificially helping others won't do it either. Only faith alone in Christ alone can secure a heavenly destiny. Have you placed your trust in Jesus Christ?

C. Our only enduring source of power is the Holy Spirit. Christ empowers all believers through the Spirit's indwelling ministry. Once we trust in Jesus for salvation, we receive the Spirit, who helps us live the Christian life (Rom. 8:10–12, 14, 26–27; Gal. 5:22–25; Eph. 1:13–14; 1 John 4:13). Are you tired of running from God, carrying the heavy weight of guilt, and living a life energized only by yourself? There's only one solution—turn to the master musician. Exchange your life for His . . . allow Him to orchestrate and perform through you what you cannot do on your own.

Living Insights

What an encouraging, liberating lesson! Living the Christian life does not mean we have to work hard to live right, but we must allow Christ to live His life through ours.

• What role does the Holy Spirit play in your life? Are you letting Him control your Christian walk? Have you died to your former fleshly nature? Read through the following Scripture passages and jot down observations that pertain to the Holy Spirit, the flesh, and you. Then take some time to consider what changes you need to make as a result of your discoveries. Bible references: Galatians 2:17–21, 5:16–18; Romans 6:1–23, 7:1–25, 8:1–17.

The Holy Spirit	
References	Observations

The Flesh	
References	Observations

You	
References	Observations

- My response to God's Word: _____

_____

_____

_____

_____

Living Insights

Study Two

We often divorce theology from practicality, limiting doctrine to the sterile surroundings of head knowledge. Our lesson contained much truth—let's make it more personal.

- In one sentence, explain what "justification in Christ" means to you.

_____

_____

_____

_____

Continued on next page

- List three ways your life is different as a direct result of your justification.

  1. _____

  2. _____

  3. _____

- Have you "died to the Law" in practice? Why or why not? Why are you no longer obligated to keep the Law?

  _____

  _____

  _____

  _____

  _____

- What does it mean to you to be "crucified with Christ"? Write Galatians 2:20 in your own words, bringing out its implications for you.

  _____

  _____

  _____

  _____

  _____

- Can you point to two or three examples of the Holy Spirit's power in your life during the past few days?

  1. _____

  2. _____

  3. _____

- Spend a few minutes talking with God. Ask for His direction and help in your areas of weakness.

Backsliding into Legalism
Galatians 3:1–9

Believers use certain words that have uniquely Christian meanings or connotations. Although unbelievers use these words too, they frequently understand them in a different light. For example, the term *saved* in Christian lingo refers to someone who has been delivered by faith in Christ from sin and everlasting punishment. To a non-Christian, however, the word conjures up images of money in a bank account or a daring rescue from some physical calamity. Similarly, in secular circles, *testimony* usually means a courtroom account of events pertinent to a trial, whereas Christians use the word to describe the story of how they came to know Christ. *Backsliding* is another term in this category. Normally, people use the word to denote a lapse into an immoral lifestyle. But it also has a distinct Christian meaning: to fall from theological truth into error.

The Galatian Christians were backsliding from the true gospel of liberty to a false gospel of legalism—a doctrine that was enslaving them to the Law of Moses. Why would they do this? What can we learn from their mistake? The first part of Galatians 3 has the answers.

I. Review of the Essentials
To help us understand and apply this timeless epistle, let's retrace the steps we have taken thus far.

A. Who is Paul? Paul is the divinely inspired writer of the letter to the first-century Galatian believers. While persecuting Christians as a zealot of Judaism, Paul was confronted by the risen Christ and appointed by Him to be an apostle and the champion of the gospel of grace to non-Jews.

B. What is legalism? Theologian Charles Ryrie makes some helpful distinctions concerning what legalism is and is not. He points out that "legalism is not the presence of laws"; otherwise, "God would have to be charged with promoting it since He has given man innumerable laws during human history."[1] Neither is legalism "the imposition of law on someone else,"[2] for if it were, God would be a legalist of the highest order. Furthermore, legalism is not the opposite of liberty, meaning that a person can live a lawless existence. As Ryrie explains, "Christian liberty does not give the believer the option of living any way he pleases; it is not license. It places him in a position where he can live as God pleases, something he was unable to do as an unregenerated

---

1. Charles Caldwell Ryrie, *Balancing the Christian Life* (Chicago, Ill.: Moody Press, 1969), p. 159.

2. Ryrie, *Balancing the Christian Life,* p. 159.

person. Liberated living is not unrestricted living."[3] What is legalism, then?

> It is a wrong attitude toward the code of laws under which a person lives. Legalism involves the presence of law, the wrong motive toward obeying that law and often the wrong use of the power provided to keep the law, but *it is basically a wrong attitude* [emphasis added]. Thus legalism may be defined as "a fleshly attitude which conforms to a code for the purpose of exalting self. . . ."

> It cannot be emphasized too strongly that *having* to do something is *not* legalism, but the wrong attitude toward doing it is.[4]

In Christian circles legalism raises its ugly head in two areas—justification and sanctification. The legalistic view of justification is "I must add to Christ's redemptive work on the cross in order for God to accept me into His family." This perspective exalts the sinful human ego to the sinless level of Christ. Sanctification, legalistically considered, is the position "I must do certain things and not do others so God and my peers will think better of me." Again, the focus is on self—on looking good rather than obeying Christ regardless of what others think. The Galatian Christians had become victims of both heresies, but Paul correctly perceives that the root of their problem was that they had accepted the legalistic doctrine of justification. Once that was cut away, the legalistic view of sanctification would wither and die.

C. **Why did the Galatian Christians backslide into legalism?** It seems incredible that people who had understood and embraced the gospel of Christian freedom would lapse into legalism. Paul is absolutely flabbergasted: "I am amazed that you are so quickly deserting Him who called you by the grace of Christ, for a different gospel; which is really not another" (Gal. 1:6–7a). Later in his letter, he conveys even greater emotion and condemnation:

> O you dear idiots of Galatia, who saw Jesus Christ the crucified so plainly, who has been casting a spell over you? I shall ask you one simple question: Did you receive the Spirit of God by trying to keep the Law or by believing the message of the Gospel? Surely you can't be so idiotic as to think that a man begins his spiritual life in the Spirit and then completes it by reverting to outward observances? Has all your

---

3. Ryrie, *Balancing the Christian Life*, p. 161.

4. Ryrie, *Balancing the Christian Life*, pp. 159–60.

painful experience brought you nowhere? I simply cannot believe it of you! (3:1–4)[5]

What caused these believers to so foolishly reverse their thinking and living? They refused to defend the Christian gospel and flirted with the legalistic teaching of the Judaizers, who led them to adopt this heresy. Paul, on the other hand, emphasizes that when he faced the false gospel of legalism, he stood strong for the truth and flatly refused to subject himself in any way to error (2:4–5, 11–16). How we need to follow Paul's example! God commands that we strive for purity in every aspect of our lives (Rom. 12:1–2, Phil. 4:8, 1 Pet. 1:13–16). But we can't even begin to reach this goal if we keep fooling around with beliefs and behaviors that lead away from true Christianity. Doing so is equivalent to a former hostage planning to return to captivity under the terrorists who once kidnapped him.[6] We cannot achieve our salvation to any degree or through any means. We are justified and sanctified through faith alone in Christ alone. There is no other way.

II. Analysis of the Argument

With this context in mind, let's consider another section of Paul's case against the legalists and his reproof of those Christians who fell prey to this counterfeit gospel.

A. Rebuke for their condition. Paul chastises the Galatian believers for committing spiritual treason, especially after having such a clear picture of the genuine gospel (Gal. 3:1). Indeed, the Greek words he uses in his rebuke for "publicly portrayed" connote the image of posting the gospel message on a public bulletin board so that no one could miss or misunderstand it. The Galatian Christians had plainly heard the truth and accepted it by faith. Yet they were now leaving it for a lie. Paul chides them for their irrational behavior, facetiously asking if they have been bewitched by a sorcerer (v. 1). We can compare the Galatian Christians to the Prodigal Son: they had left everything of real value behind to live on their own and, as a result, ended up in

---

5. J. B. Phillips, *The New Testament in Modern English,* rev. ed. (New York, N.Y.: The Macmillan Co., 1972), p. 403.

6. This point does not negate our need to understand false teaching so that we can avoid accepting it, refute it, and help others from becoming its victims (Acts 17:1–4, 16–34; 2 Cor. 10:5; Titus 1:9–14; Jude 3–4). As two Christian scholars correctly observe: "A Christian must recognize error before he can counter it, just as a doctor must study disease before he can knowledgeably treat it. The Christian church has on occasion been penetrated by false teaching precisely because Christians have not adequately been trained to detect the 'disease' of error" (Norman L. Geisler and Paul D. Feinberg, *Introduction to Philosophy: A Christian Perspective* [Grand Rapids, Mich.: Baker Book House, 1980], p. 73).

the pigpen of human works, spiritually insane (Luke 15:11–17; compare Prov. 18:1).

B. Reasons for their error. Paul goes on to spell out why the Galatian believers were wrong to choose works over faith.

   1. Their choice contradicted their salvation experience. Paul asks them if they had become Christians by works or by faith (Gal. 3:2). Of course, they knew it was faith in Jesus Christ that had brought them into God's family. So Paul asks if they were now trying to earn what they had already received by faith. The Holy Spirit had regenerated them, and He was rejuvenating them (vv. 3–5). How could they possibly do anything to improve on the Spirit's work? The idea was absurd! It would be like driving a car, knowing it is fueled by gas, only to later accept the claim that the car runs better when pushed.

   2. Their choice contradicted the Old Testament's doctrine of salvation. Paul masterfully turns from the Galatians' experience of salvation to Abraham's. This Old Testament patriarch was the father of the Jews. If works could save, then Abraham must have been saved by them. But Paul points out that Abraham was justified by faith alone:

   > Even so Abraham believed God, and it was reck-
   > oned to him as righteousness. Therefore, be sure
   > that it is those who are of faith who are sons of
   > Abraham. And the Scripture, foreseeing that God
   > would justify the Gentiles by faith, preached the
   > gospel beforehand to Abraham, saying, "All the
   > nations shall be blessed in you." So then those
   > who are of faith are blessed with Abraham, the
   > believer. (vv. 6–9)

   Faith was, is, and always will be the only way to become rightly related to God. Not a halfhearted faith, but a total trust that says, "I stake my life now and forever on the sufficiency of Christ's death to reconcile me to God. Everything else is superfluous."

III. Lessons from the Message

Paul's hard-hitting assessment of and argument against doctrinal backsliding leaves us with three final lessons we dare not ignore.

A. Legalism is an aggressive enemy; don't make friends with it. Resist the temptation to exalt yourself in any aspect of salvation. God deserves all the credit for everyone's justification, sanctification, and glorification—including yours.

B. Backsliding is temporary insanity; don't attempt to reason with it. Some of the most irrational people are backsliders. You can't reason with them about their condition, because they have temporarily lost their senses. But you can pray for them and love them—they sorely need both.

C. Salvation is free; don't try to earn it. Grace holds out her hand, offering complete forgiveness and restoration if you'll only take it. You can't buy it—it has already been purchased by Jesus Christ. And now God offers it freely to you. Have you taken it? If not, will you do so today?

 Living Insights

Study One ▬▬▬▬▬▬▬▬▬▬▬▬▬▬▬▬▬▬▬▬▬▬▬▬▬▬▬▬

Paul's reference to Abraham was a master stroke against the legalists. The father of the Jews is one of the finest examples of righteousness by faith. A closer look will help us see this even more clearly.

● Paul discusses Abraham's faith in two places—Galatians 3:6–9 and Romans 4:1–5. We need to clarify several words in these two passages. Using a Bible dictionary, Bible encyclopedia, or theology book, define the following terms in words you understand.

Justified (Rom. 4:2, Gal. 3:8): _____

_____

_____

Works (Rom. 4:2): _____

_____

_____

Believed (Rom. 4:3, Gal. 3:6): _____

_____

_____

Reckoned (Rom. 4:3, Gal. 3:6): _____

_____

_____

Continued on next page

Righteousness (Rom. 4:3, Gal. 3:6): _____

_____

_____

Wage (Rom. 4:4): _____

_____

_____

Favor (Rom. 4:4): _____

_____

_____

Ungodly (Rom. 4:5): _____

_____

_____

Faith (Gal. 3:7–9): _____

_____

_____

Blessed (Gal. 3:8–9): _____

_____

_____

🌳 *Living Insights*

Study Two ▬▬▬▬▬▬▬▬▬▬▬▬▬▬▬▬▬▬▬

Backsliding into legalism is not a pleasant picture, but it's one that needs to be painted and made personal. Maybe you know a backslider or a legalist. Perhaps it's *you*. Carefully consider the following questions.

• How is it possible to "make friends" with legalism? Think of specific ways it subtly creeps into our lives.

_____

_____

_____

_____

_____

_____

_____

_____

_____

_____

- Has backsliding entered your life? If so, how do you plan to deal with it? What have you learned from this lesson that will help your strategy?

_____

_____

_____

_____

_____

_____

_____

_____

Delivered from a Curse

Galatians 3:10–14

Some of life's issues are either/or rather than both/and. For instance, you're either married or single. You can't be both at the same time. Similarly, salvation is either by faith or by works. There are no alternatives, and these are mutually exclusive—they cannot be mixed because they are poles apart. Add even one deed of human effort to salvation, and you pass from faith to works . . . from grace to Law . . . from a divine gift to a human wage. More than that, you move from life to death, from being blessed to being condemned. The Apostle Paul develops and defends this last point in Galatians 3:10–14. He responds to the legalists' position that we can be accepted by God through obedience to the Old Testament Law. Through Paul we learn that Christianity is a religion of "done," and that all other faiths are religions of "do." We also discover that Christianity leads to divine favor; all other paths dead-end in divine judgment.

I. Two Ways to Approach God

In Paul's day the Judaizers believed that divine grace and human achievement brought a righteous standing before God. They also taught that a mixture of faith and works was necessary for a person to remain in this favorable position. In other words, justification and sanctification were tied together by human trust and effort. Paul challenges this heresy, arguing that only grace through faith is necessary for both justification and sanctification. Certainly, works will come as the fruit of faith, but they are not needed to win God's approval. His declaration, "I accept you," has nothing to do with man's effort; it never could. Why is this so? Paul answers by explaining two ways to approach God—one by works and the other by faith.

A. By the works of the Law. Paul writes, "As many as are of the works of the Law are under a curse" (Gal. 3:10a). Those who choose to gain God's approval by keeping the demands of the Mosaic Law fall under the Law's condemnation. Why? Because, as the Law itself states, " 'Cursed is everyone who does not abide by *all things* written in the book of the Law, to perform them' " (v. 10b, emphasis added; compare Deut. 27:26–28:1). The only way to win God's favor through obedience to the Law is to keep every aspect of it. But no one except Jesus Christ has ever done so. Indeed, no one ever could measure up to God's perfect standard without being born with a sin-free nature. And since every human being, as a consequence of man's fall (Gen. 3), comes into this world with a propensity to sin, not one has been able to obey every command of the Law. Therefore, those who try to live under the Law sentence themselves to death. This is why the Law was designed—God gave it to man to reveal his inability to keep it. As Paul says in Romans 3: "Whatever the Law says, it speaks to those who are under the Law, that every mouth may be closed, and all the world may become accountable to God; because by the works of the Law no flesh will be justified in His sight; for through the Law comes the knowledge of sin" (vv. 19–20). So the road to God via law-keeping, or works, ends not in divine pleasure but in divine wrath. The Law shows we are sinners who deserve God's justice and desperately need His mercy.

B. By faith apart from works. The second avenue to God is through faith alone: "Now that no one is justified by the Law before God is evident; for, 'The righteous man shall live by faith.' However, the Law is not of faith; on the contrary, 'He who practices them shall live by them'" (Gal. 3:11–12). Seeking justification by faith and by the Law is a costly mistake. It's like lacing a cool glass of lemonade with cyanide—no matter how refreshing the lemonade may taste, the poison will surely kill you. However, we who live by trusting in Christ rather than ourselves freely receive the Father's declaration of full forgiveness and unreserved acceptance. How can this be? Because, as Paul explains, "Christ redeemed us from the curse of the Law, having become a curse for us—for it is written, 'Cursed is everyone who hangs on a tree'" (v. 13). The basis for Paul's statement is found in Deuteronomy—the fifth book of the Law. In ancient Israel, criminals sentenced to death and executed were to be hung on trees as symbols of God's judgment (21:22–23). Since we all have committed sins worthy of the spiritual death sentence, we, too, deserve to be killed and hung on a tree. Knowing this, God sent His Son to be conceived in a virgin, assuring He would be born with a sinless human nature (Matt. 1:18–25).[1] The Son's mission was to obey the Law perfectly, thus fulfilling it, and to die in our place on a wooden cross, paying the debt we owed (5:17–19, 16:21; Mark 10:45). Our guilt and punishment were transferred to Christ, the innocent one, whose death freed us from the Law's curse. He has accomplished everything necessary for our salvation. We can add nothing to it; all we can do is receive or reject His complete payment, pardon, and restoration.

II. Answers to Three Questions

The apostle's argument in Galatians 3:10–14 often raises three questions. Let's examine each one.

A. How could God's Law curse anyone? Isn't the Lord loving, compassionate, and merciful? How could such a God institute

---

1. See *The Virgin Birth: Doctrine of Deity,* by Robert G. Gromacki (1974; reprint, Grand Rapids, Mich.: Baker Book House, 1981), chap. 13.

a legal code that would lead to the condemnation of the human race? The problem seems irreconcilable. And it is, as long as one ignores God's holiness, righteousness, and justice and assumes an anemic view of God. Bible expositor John Stott puts it well:

> There is no need to be embarrassed by these outspoken words [of cursing]. They express what Scripture everywhere tells us about God in relation to sin, namely that no man can sin with impunity, for God is not a sentimental old Father Christmas, but the righteous Judge of men. Disobedience always brings us under the curse of God, and exposes us to the awful penalties of His judgment. . . . So if the blessing of God brings justification and life, the curse of God brings condemnation and death.[2]

B. What does "Christ redeemed us from the curse" mean? The Greek word for *redeem* means "to buy out of slavery." Because we are conceived, born, and involved in sin, we are enslaved to it, unable to free ourselves from its stranglehold. Understanding our helpless condition, Christ mercifully paid the only acceptable price for our release—He substituted His own perfect life for our imperfect ones (Acts 20:28, Col. 2:13–14, 1 Pet. 1:18–19). In doing so, He satisfied God's justice and lifted from our heads the Law's curse of death.

C. Why isn't everyone automatically saved? After all, if Christ has paid our penalty, hasn't everyone passed from death to life? No, because not everyone has freely accepted His payment for their sin. Only those who have are "in Christ Jesus"; they have been born again into God's forever family and are recipients of "the promise of the Spirit through faith" (Gal. 3:14). All others who are outside of Christ are doomed by the curse of the Law. If we are not in Him, we are still trying to pay a debt Christ has already paid. We are, in effect, slapping Christ in the face, living as if He had done nothing at all or not enough to liberate us. Therefore, we are still living by works, trying to earn God's favor through our own efforts. This leaves us under the Law's death sentence. We are like criminals sitting on death row, refusing a complete pardon on the grounds that we can discover a better way to escape the gas chamber.

III. Two Principles Worth Applying

Paul's message from these few verses in Galatians 3 provides a couple of principles we need to weigh carefully.

---

2. John R. W. Stott, *The Message of Galatians: Only One Way,* The Bible Speaks Today series (Downers Grove, Ill.: InterVarsity Press, 1968), p. 79.

A. Salvation is an either/or proposition. Either we accept God's salvation gift by faith alone, or we don't accept it at all. There are no alternatives in the Savior's eyes. Of course, we can be saved without knowing about or even understanding other facets of Christianity. But we cannot become righteous before God without believing that Jesus Christ died in our place and rose from the dead so we might have everlasting life. Do you believe this? Have you made Him the center of your life by faith alone? If not, you are still on death row, awaiting everlasting torment in hell.

B. Deliverance from the Law's curse depends on Christ, not us. To be saved, we cannot do anything but put our trust in Jesus and His finished work on the cross. Is faith, then, a work? Is it an act added to Christ's death that brings us salvation? No— faith is merely receiving with empty hands what Christ supplies completely. As Stott again so aptly expresses it:

> Faith is laying hold of Jesus Christ personally. There is no merit in it. It is not another 'work.' Its value is not in itself, but entirely in its object, Jesus Christ. As Luther put it, 'faith ... apprehendeth nothing else but that precious jewel Christ Jesus.' Christ is the Bread of life; faith feeds upon Him. Christ was lifted up on the cross; faith gazes at Him there.[3]

Secure in Christ

If you have trusted Christ by faith, you are in Him, forever freed from the curse of the Law. You will never have to seek God's favor. He is completely satisfied with His Son, and since you are in Him, God is completely satisfied with you as well. He may not always like what you do with your freedom, but He will never turn His back on you (Heb. 13:5–6). You are secure in Him for eternity (John 10:27–30). Now praise Him for His mercy and use your freedom to honor Him.

Continued on next page

3. Stott, *The Message of Galatians*, p. 82.

🐎 *Living Insights*

Once again the Apostle Paul conveys his message in strong terms. Work equals curse. Faith equals righteousness. Salvation is clearly black or white; there's no room for gray.

● A question frequently heard is, What's the value of works, anyway? Do we need them? What does Scripture say? Let's do a little New Testament study on works. Read each verse listed below to determine if it refers to works *before* salvation or works *as a result of* salvation. Circle the appropriate response, then write down the value of works as discussed in each verse.

The Value of Works

Matthew 5:16   Before / After Salvation

Value: _____

_____

John 6:27   Before / After Salvation

Value: _____

_____

John 6:28–29   Before / After Salvation

Value: _____

_____

Romans 2:14–15   Before / After Salvation

Value: _____

_____

Romans 3:20   Before / After Salvation

Value: _____

_____

Romans 3:28   Before / After Salvation

Value: _____

_____

1 Corinthians 3:10–14   Before / After Salvation

Value: _____

_____

1 Corinthians 3:15   Before / After Salvation

Value: _____

_____

Galatians 2:16   Before / After Salvation

Value: _____

_____

Ephesians 2:8–9   Before / After Salvation

Value: _____

_____

Philippians 2:12–13   Before / After Salvation

Value: _____

_____

Colossians 1:9–10   Before / After Salvation

Value: _____

_____

1 Timothy 6:18   Before / After Salvation

Value: _____

_____

Hebrews 6:1   Before / After Salvation

Value: _____

_____

James 2:14–20   Before / After Salvation

Value: _____

_____

Continued on next page

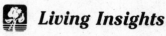 *Living Insights*

We learned in this lesson that the *work* of salvation has all been done by God so we could have it as a *gift*. If these words are commonplace to you, stop and reread them slowly, reflecting on their meaning.

- God has provided salvation as a gift. Have you received this gift by faith? If not, will you do so now? If you have already, how long has it been since you've thanked God for His indescribable gift? Let's spend our time today writing God a thank-you note. Try to express your true feelings through your writing. Think about the curse under which you lived, the deliverance Christ provided, the price He paid for your release, and the results that followed. All too often we forget to thank Him for what He had to sacrifice in order to give us life. You can begin to remedy that right now.

Dear heavenly Father,

_____

_____

_____

_____

_____

_____

_____

_____

_____

_____

_____

Your grateful child,

_____

Three Men and a Promise
Galatians 3:15–22

If history proves anything, it is that we seldom learn what it teaches. For example, the history of the Roman Empire shows us that sexual promiscuity and other forms of self-indulgence lead to the internal decay and eventual downfall of nations. Yet we continue to allow immorality to spread like a cancerous growth, hoping against hope that it will simply go away on its own.[1]

History also points out that political power never operates in a religious vacuum. If Christianity doesn't fill the void, lawmakers and policy setters will find, or even create, another religion to take its place. This fact, however, doesn't seem to motivate many Christians to enter the political arena or base their civil decisions on their faith.[2]

Similarly, the ruins of past civilizations stand as stark reminders that human beings are unable to perfect themselves regardless of their economic, political, educational, or religious achievements. And yet many people insist that their utopian dreams rest in their own hands.[3] During the first century, the Judaizers failed to consider accurately the historical record concerning the way man can become right before God. They looked at the Mosaic Law, misunderstood its function, and declared that obedience to its commands would bring salvation. They ignored the fact that everyone stood condemned, not justified, under the Law's perfect standard. They also disregarded the fact that prior to the Law, God made a promise to Abraham that was not dependent on his keeping a set of rules. Abraham was saved by believing in this promise, and we are saved by believing in God's fulfillment of this promise. Let's avoid the mistakes the Judaizers made and focus our thoughts on Paul's history lesson in Galatians 3:15–22. We will observe the solid, historical fact of justification by faith alone in contrast to the perilous fiction of justification by works.

I. The Historical Background
Before turning our attention to Galatians, we need to dig into the pages of history, beginning with the days of Abraham.

1. See *Our Dance Has Turned to Death,* by Carl W. Wilson (Atlanta, Ga.: Renewal Publishing Co., 1979); and *Whatever Happened to the Human Race?* by Francis A. Schaeffer and C. Everett Koop (Old Tappan, N.J.: Fleming H. Revell Co., 1979).

2. See *The Naked Public Square: Religion and Democracy in America,* by Richard John Neuhaus (Grand Rapids, Mich.: William B. Eerdmans Publishing Co., 1984).

3. See *Is Man the Measure? An Evaluation of Contemporary Humanism,* by Norman L. Geisler (Grand Rapids, Mich.: Baker Book House, 1983); and *Unmasking the New Age,* by Douglas R. Groothuis (Downers Grove, Ill.: InterVarsity Press, 1986).

A. Abraham. Some two thousand years before Jesus' birth, God appeared to Abraham and told him,

> "I will make you a great nation,
> And I will bless you,
> And make your name great;
> And so you shall be a blessing;
> And I will bless those who bless you,
> And the one who curses you I will curse.
> And in you all the families of the earth shall be
> blessed." (Gen. 12:2–3)

On several occasions the Lord repeated His promise to Abraham, saying at one juncture, " 'I will greatly multiply your *seed* as the stars of the heavens, and as the sand which is on the seashore; and your *seed* shall possess the gate of their enemies. And in your *seed* all the nations of the earth shall be blessed' " (22:17–18a, emphasis added). The fact that "seed" is singular is crucial, as we'll soon see. But for now, the important point is that God's promise was unconditional. Abraham didn't have to do anything to make it come about. By simply believing in God's ability to fulfill His promise, Abraham was declared righteous by the Lord (15:1–6). And regardless of what Abraham thought or did, the promise was irrevocable. God made it; He would bring it to pass.

B. Moses. Following Abraham's death, the Lord continued to remind the patriarch's descendants of His promise (26:3–4, 24; 28:13–15; 35:11–12). Eventually, however, the Hebrews found themselves helplessly enslaved in Egypt. Having compassion on their plight, the Lord sent Moses to them and worked through him to deliver the people from oppression (Exod. 1–15). After the Exodus, God revealed the Law to Moses, demanding that the Hebrews make it their standard for living (20:1–31:18). Realizing they would not be able to keep it, the Lord included a system of sacrifices designed to bring forgiveness to those who used it by faith.[4]

C. Christ. In his letter to the Galatian Christians, Paul argues that Jesus' self-sacrifice on Calvary set all people free from the Law's condemnation. When we place our faith in Christ, we are unshackled from the curse of the Law and given a new lease on life (Gal. 3:10–14). The Judaizers gagged on this gospel of grace. They could stand fitting Christ and faith into the salvation plan but not without including obedience to the Law. In their minds the demands of the Law superseded the promise made to Abraham.

---

4. See "Salvation in the Old Testament," by John S. Feinberg, in *Tradition and Testament: Essays in Honor of Charles Lee Feinberg*, ed. John S. Feinberg and Paul D. Feinberg (Chicago, Ill.: Moody Press, 1981), pp. 59–75.

Perhaps Abraham was saved by faith, they thought, but with the initiation of the Law came a new way to be made right before God. From that point on, salvation included rule-keeping.

II. An Expositional Analysis

Paul challenges this legalistic viewpoint in Galatians 3:15–22. He maintains that the promise to Abraham was not annulled by the Law; rather, the Law demonstrated the need for the promise.

A. The Law did not annul the promise (vv. 15–18). Paul begins his argument with an illustration drawn from everyday life: "Just as no one can set aside or add to a human covenant that has been duly established, so it is in this case" (v. 15)[5]—the case of the covenant God made to Abraham. Imagine that you have written a will that has been approved by a licensed probate attorney. In the will, you specify who will get what and when. Soon after your death, selected family members and friends gather together to hear your will read. Some are pleased by what they hear; others are surprised, disappointed, and even infuriated. The will can be contested, but no one can alter or annul its terms as long as it is demonstrated that you had full control of your mental faculties when you made it. Now if a human's will can't be revised or revoked, how much more immutable and indestructible is a promise made by the eternal God. The promise Paul has in mind is the one made to Abraham concerning "his seed" (v. 16a). Paul astutely observes, "[God] does not say, 'And to seeds,' as referring to many, but rather to one, 'And to your seed,' that is, Christ" (v. 16b). From God's perspective, the ultimate fulfillment of His covenant with Abraham went beyond establishing the Hebrews in the Promised Land. It included blessing all the families of the earth, regardless of their national or racial heritage. And this blessing, this divine inheritance, is salvation by faith in *Christ,* no one else. Through Him, everyone can become spiritual descendants of Abraham—"heirs according to promise" (v. 29). How does all this relate to the Law?

> The Law, which came four hundred and thirty years [after the promise], does not invalidate a covenant previously ratified by God, so as to nullify the promise. For if the inheritance is based on law, it is no longer based on a promise; but God has granted it to Abraham by means of a promise. (vv. 17–18)

That is, God's promise was unconditional; it came with no strings attached. So when the Law was revealed and implemented, it

---

5. *The NIV Study Bible* (Grand Rapids, Mich.: Zondervan Bible Publishers, 1985).

did not annul or change the promise. Both existed side by side, neither impinging on the other.

B. The Law made the promise essential (vv. 19–22). Paul's conclusion raises two questions: one regards the Law's purpose, and the other concerns the Law's possible conflict with the Abrahamic promise.

    1. "Why the Law then?" If the Law didn't affect the promise, why was it given? We needed it, Paul says, "Because of transgressions" (v. 19a). Before the Law, our final court of appeal for right and wrong was our own conscience (Rom. 2:14–15), and its judgments were relatively easy to ignore or explain away. But the Law clearly defined what was moral and immoral, godly and ungodly. Sin was no longer a matter of human opinion, but divinely established fact. Now we knew we were transgressors of God's righteous standard, not simply offenders of human law (compare 3:20, 4:15, 7:7). Put briefly, the Mosaic Law's function was not to provide salvation but to convince us of our need for salvation. If we ever doubt we're sinners, all we have to do is look at the Old Testament Law and start checking off the commands we have broken. It won't take long before we realize that we're sinners in need of the Savior. Paul adds that the Law came to the Hebrews thirdhand: from God to angels to Moses, the mediator to the people (Gal. 3:19b). The promise of salvation, however, was directly given by God to Abraham (v. 20). It was unilateral and unconditional; unlike the Law, which was mediated and dependent on man's obedience.[6] Therefore, the promise was superior to the Law—the Law served the promise, not vice versa.

    2. "Is the Law then contrary to the promises of God?" Does the gospel oppose or contradict the Law of Moses? "May it never be! For if a law had been given which was able to impart life, then righteousness would indeed have been based on law. But the Scripture has shut up all men under sin, that the promise by faith in Jesus Christ might be given to those who believe" (vv. 21–22). On a purely hypothetical level, if God had given a law by which people could be saved, then people could have been made righteous on the basis of that law. But God never gave such a law. Instead, He revealed an ethical standard that exposed people's sin and their inability to obey the Lord completely. This Law actually drove them to the promise of salvation by faith.

6. See "Galatians," by James Montgomery Boice, in *The Expositor's Bible Commentary,* 12 vols., ed. Frank E. Gaebelein (Grand Rapids, Mich.: Zondervan Publishing House, 1976), vol. 10, p. 465.

Seen in this light, the Law was actually an expression of God's grace, pointing the way to the ultimate fulfillment of the Abrahamic promise in Christ.

III. The Practical Significance

We would be remiss if we allowed this tightly woven historical and theological argument to remain on the pages of Scripture. Let's cut it out and stitch it as an integral part of the fabric of our lives.

A. The protection of grace is not altered by the demands of the Law. The Law shouts at us, "Guilty! Judged! Condemned!" while the promise proclaims, "This is the way to complete forgiveness and full reconciliation with God." Do you realize that apart from Christ you stand convicted as a sinner and doomed to damnation? You cannot please God on your own; you can only incite His wrath. Yet this fact does not harm His plan of salvation in any way. In fact, it shows how desperately you need to drink of His redemptive grace, if you haven't already. Will you move from being under the Law to being under Christ? He is waiting, ready to welcome you and quench your thirst.

B. The greater the demands of condemnation, the sweeter the promise of salvation. You will never fully appreciate the gospel of grace until you have seen yourself against the backdrop of the Law.

> Not until the law has bruised and smitten us will we admit our need of the gospel to bind up our wounds. Not until the law has arrested and imprisoned us will we pine for Christ to set us free. Not until the law has condemned and killed us will we call upon Christ for justification and life. Not until the law has driven us to despair of ourselves will we ever believe in Jesus. Not until the law has humbled us even to hell will we turn to the gospel to raise us to heaven.[7]

Take some time out this week to read the Law—try Deuteronomy. Pay particular attention to its emphasis on perfection ... holiness ... total obedience. See how you stack up. As the oppression mounts, remember the fulfillment of the Abrahamic promise: God's richest blessings are available to you through Christ. Give yourself to Him; He will give you back His best.

Continued on next page

---

7. John R. W. Stott, *The Message of Galatians: Only One Way,* The Bible Speaks Today series (Downers Grove, Ill.: InterVarsity Press, 1968), p. 93.

Living Insights

Study One ▬▬▬▬▬▬▬▬▬▬▬▬▬▬▬▬▬▬

The Law and its purpose are starting to take on their proper perspective. By reviewing history, Paul is able to give us a better understanding of what the Law can and cannot do.

- Did you catch all the significance woven through this passage of Galatians? One fine way to increase understanding is to read through the verses and paraphrase them. You may find this method a great help in making the text more personal. Paraphrase Galatians 3:15–22 and then begin to apply what you've learned in this lesson.

Galatians 3:15–22

_____

_____

_____

_____

_____

_____

_____

_____

_____

_____

_____

_____

_____

_____

_____

_____

Living Insights

This history lesson teaches us that God blessed all mankind through His promise to Abraham. We also see that to add the Law to this promise is to put a condition on a promise that was unconditional. Let's center our thoughts on the idea of God's promise.

• What does *unconditional* mean? Write out a concise, clear definition.

_____

_____

• Jot down the conditions you frequently hear for salvation.

_____

_____

_____

• List the things many people do to keep their salvation.

_____

_____

_____

• How does all of this contradict the unconditional aspect of salvation?

_____

_____

• Are you guilty of distorting God's unconditional salvation? Are you tagging on conditions for keeping your salvation? Think about it and talk with God about what you've learned.

Preempting the Paidagogos
Galatians 3:23–29

In the ancient world of the Roman Empire, the social structure and economy were dependent on slave labor.

> Work done by slaves ranged the gamut of occupations from factory work and mining to medicine, from farming to business management, from cooking to teaching. Some slaves even acted as secretaries to the administrators of the empire, rising to important positions of high responsibility before being freed to become useful additions to the higher echelons of the citizenry. . . . To put it crudely, but not inaccurately, slaves were the machines of their day.[1]

Philosophically, slaves were acknowledged as human beings, but legally, they were regarded as things—commercial assets to be owned. As such, slaves were under the authority of their masters, obligated to fulfill their wishes to the fullest extent possible. Furthermore, the masters controlled their physical well-being. Although Roman law provided some protection from abuse, owners could severely chastise or even kill their slaves. In short, slaves were completely under their masters' power until their freedom could be attained.[2]

Likewise, the Apostle Paul argues in Galatians that we are enslaved to sin and under the deadly curse of the Law. Unless our liberation is secured, we are doomed to serve evil now and in hell. But, Paul exclaims, our freedom has been purchased—paid by the blood of God's own Son, Jesus Christ. We can breathe freedom's fresh air if we will just accept Christ's payment by faith alone. In the latter section of Galatians 3, Paul continues to unveil this gospel of grace, showing us how the Law led us to freedom in Christ.

I. Under the Law: In Bondage
During the period of the Law, from the days of Moses to the ascension of Christ, what was the Law's purpose? If it wasn't given as a means to justification, what was its function? Paul answers through two metaphors.

A. A prison. "Before faith came," Paul writes, "we were kept in custody under the law, being shut up to the faith which was

1. Francis Lyall, *Slaves, Citizens, Sons: Legal Metaphors in the Epistles* (Grand Rapids, Mich.: Zondervan Publishing House, 1984), p. 27.

2. For more information on slavery in Bible times, see the entry "Slave, Slavery" by A. Rupprecht in *The Zondervan Pictorial Encyclopedia of the Bible* (Grand Rapids, Mich.: Zondervan Publishing House, 1976), vol. 5, pp. 453–60; and the study guide *New Testament Postcards*, coauthored by Ken Gire, Jr., from the Bible-teaching ministry of Charles R. Swindoll (Fullerton, Calif.: Insight for Living, 1986), pp. 1–10.

later to be revealed" (Gal. 3:23). The Greek verb translated "kept in custody" means "to protect by military guards." John Stott explains that "when [this term was] applied to a city, it was used both of keeping the enemy out and of keeping the inhabitants in, lest they should flee or desert."[3] Another verb in the verse, translated "shut up," carries the idea of hemming in or cooping up. Considered together, these verbs convey the thought that the Law was our prison, confining us as criminals who had violated its precepts, thereby bringing us under its curse. We lived behind bars, condemned to death because we were sinners ... lawbreakers ... rebels against God's perfect standard of righteousness. The Law was a constant reminder of our miserable condition before God.

B. A guardian. The other metaphor Paul uses is *paidagōgos*, translated "tutor" in some versions of the Bible (v. 24a). The term does not denote a teacher but refers to "a child-custodian, child-attendant." The paidagogos was usually a slave whose duty was to escort the master's children to and from school and to oversee their behavior. This strict disciplinarian was "often harsh to the point of cruelty, and [was] usually depicted in ancient drawings with a rod or cane in his hand."[4] Prior to Christ's redemptive work, the Law was our guardian, warning us to stay on the straight and narrow, punishing us when we strayed, and protecting us until we arrived at our divinely intended destination—justification by faith in God's Son (v. 24b).

II. In Christ: Sons of God

Now that Jesus Christ has been revealed as our Savior, and we have placed our faith in Him, what is our relationship to the Law? Are we still under its watchful eye and wretched curse? Praise God—no! "Now that faith has come, we are no longer under a tutor" (v. 25). Through our belief in Christ, our prison door has been opened and our paidagogos has been retired. We are free ... gloriously free! But where does that leave us? Are we now alone in the world, forced to fend for ourselves? Not at all. As Paul explains, we have become new members of God's family, united in equality, heirs of an ancient promise. Let's probe each of these practical truths.

A. Members of God's family. "[We] are all sons of God through faith in Christ Jesus" (v. 26). There are no exceptions. All who trust in Christ as their Redeemer become full-fledged members of God's everlasting family. Of course, without faith in Jesus, no one can have an intimate relationship with the Lord. The only

3. John R. W. Stott, *The Message of Galatians: Only One Way,* The Bible Speaks Today series (Downers Grove, Ill.: InterVarsity Press, 1968), p. 96.

4. Stott, *The Message of Galatians,* p. 97.

way to the Father is through His Son (John 14:6), and the only way to the Son is by faith in Him. But once we're in Jesus, we are so identified with Him that we are immersed in Him and clothed with Him (Gal. 3:27). We don't become Christ, but we do begin to become *like* Him, until the day we stand before our Father, Christlike through and through (Rom. 8:29–30, Col. 3:1–4, 1 Thess. 5:23, 1 John 3:2). And none of us who trust in Christ will ever be removed from God's family. Once sons, always sons. Our adoption is irrevocable.

B. Members of one another. In Christ, we are united not only to God but also to all other believers. "[We] are all one in Christ Jesus" (Gal. 3:28b). Paul specifies three results of our Christian unity. In doing so, he doesn't deny our individuality—instead, he points out that the distinctions that once divided us have been made obsolete by Christ. He has torn down the walls we built to separate ourselves from each other. Now we are free to fellowship with one another as brothers and sisters.

1. **No distinction of race.** "There is neither Jew nor Greek" (v. 28a). All racial distinctions and prejudices are meaningless in the Body of Christ. We are equal, regardless of our heritage, skin color, or language (compare Eph. 2:11–22).

2. **No distinction of rank.** "There is neither slave nor free man" (Gal. 3:28a). No one gets special favors or benefits based on social status. Wealthy or poor, educated or uneducated, management or labor, nobility or servants ... it doesn't matter. In Christ, we're all on the same level.

3. **No distinction of sex.** "There is neither male nor female" (v. 28b). In Paul's day, women were badly treated. They were considered by Jew and Gentile alike to be inferior to men and little better than common slaves. Indeed, a morning prayer for a Jewish male often included a statement of thanks to God that "Thou hast not made me a Gentile, a slave or a woman."[5] The gospel strikes at the very heart of this viewpoint, making all people equal in Christ.

C. Members of Abraham's family. Our union with Christ also makes us spiritual children of Abraham—the father of Israel and all who come to God by faith (v. 29; compare vv. 6–7). We join the ranks of all the people who believed before us. Because of our adoption into this well-established family, "no longer do we feel ourselves to be waifs and strays, without any significance in history, or bits of useless flotsam drifting on the tide of time.

---

5. As quoted by William Barclay in *The Letters to the Galatians and Ephesians,* rev. ed. (Philadelphia, Pa.: The Westminster Press, 1976), p. 32.

Instead, we find our place in the unfolding purpose of God."[6] We discover our identity as it was meant to be: children of God destined for a heavenly home of everlasting happiness and celebration.

III. Some Reasons to Praise Our God

Galatians 3:23–29 is the most upbeat portion of Paul's letter we've studied so far. In keeping with its spirit, let's turn our application into words of praise.

A. Praise God for the prison. The Law brought us to the end of ourselves, forcing us to face our condition squarely. Let's thank the Lord for providing this humanly inescapable penitentiary. Without it, we may never have realized how much we needed His grace.

B. Praise God for the guardian. Like the paidagogos of old, the Law helped keep us in line, restraining sin while it guided us toward our liberator—Christ the Lord. Let's express our appreciation to God for giving us this goad to salvation.

C. Praise God for the Savior. With His own blood, Christ made it possible for us to become united with the Father and all believers past, present, and future. Through faith we have been set free to serve and enjoy the living God. Let's not take our redemption for granted—rather, let's turn our eyes toward heaven and, with humble gratitude, praise Christ for what He has done for us.

 Living Insights

Study One

One of the distinctions of the Body of Christ is that it should be free from prejudice. Galatians 3:28 tells us that we "are all one in Christ Jesus." Have you given much consideration to God's equal acceptance of all?

- Like Galatians 3:28, 1 Corinthians 12:12–27 is a look at equality in the Church. But unlike Galatians, the Corinthian passage discusses functional diversity within essential equality; we are equally God's children even though we are gifted to perform different tasks. As you read through these verses, look for principles of equality and note them in the chart on the following page.

Continued on next page

6. Stott, *The Message of Galatians,* p. 101.

1 Corinthians 12:12–27	
Verses	Principles of Equality

 Living Insights

Our lesson concluded with an expression of praise. Let's hitchhike on that idea and continue with some worshipful reflection.

- *Praise God for the prison.* Can you recall a "prison" or two in your life? Do you find it tough to give God praise for those circumstances? What did it feel like to come to the end of yourself? What values do you have as a result of your prison experiences?
- *Praise God for the guardian.* We've been pretty hard on the Law so far. But it did play a vital part in our lives, didn't it? Can you see how the Law was instrumental in leading you to Christ? Reflect on that and offer praise to God.
- *Praise God for the Savior.* If you know the Savior, you have no better reason to praise Him than the fact that He is your Savior. If you don't know Christ, will you accept Him now? Will you escape the bondage of sin? Join believers in praising God for the Savior.

No Longer a Slave—a Son!

Galatians 4:1–11

By the ripe old age of seventeen, she had been in and out of juvenile hall and the city jail more times than she could remember. She had tried to obey the rules at home—but there were so many of them. "You must do this and this and this . . . don't forget about this . . . and for goodness' sake, don't do that or that or that"; the list went on and on. With every rule kept came a smile or "Good girl"; with every law broken came an exacting and inescapable punishment. Her parents were consistent—for that she gave them credit. But they were also tightfisted, demanding, domineering, and unmerciful.

The strain of living at home eventually became too great. She ran away at the age of twelve . . . then again when she was thirteen . . . once more at fifteen. While on her own, she explored her "freedom" through drugs, prostitution, burglary, and a dozen other crimes. She landed respectable jobs from time to time but couldn't keep them for long. Try as she might, she couldn't meet her parents' or society's demands. Consequently, social workers, police officers, pimps, and dope dealers became her foster parents. And they all believed her lifestyle would soon kill her. She believed that too, but she couldn't see any way out. She thought she didn't deserve anything better. All she heard in her head were the pounding words "You're trapped, guilty, doomed." She desperately needed someone to rescue her—someone to do what neither she nor anyone else could: provide forgiveness and strength to live a genuinely free life.

In many respects, we are like this teenage girl. Perhaps we haven't rebelled in the same ways. Yet all of us have broken rules, not just our parents' or society's, but God's as well. And we all have despaired of living up to the expectations and standards of others. Our disobedience has resulted in the divine judge's gavel coming down to proclaim us guilty; our sentence, death. Our only hope is a rescuer . . . a savior . . . someone who will do for us what no one else can.

The good news of Galatians is that the judge Himself has provided us with such a person: His Son, Jesus Christ. How merciful! How self-giving! We can be set free. Indeed, as Paul explains in Galatians 4:1–11, our freedom comes with adoption papers—papers that tell us our new father is God and our new source of strength is the Holy Spirit.

I. Our Condition under the Law

Throughout much of Galatians, Paul says a great deal about our condition under the Mosaic Law. In the beginning of chapter 4, he continues to expand on this theme, though he takes it in a somewhat different direction.

A. The illustration. "Now I say, as long as the heir is a child, he does not differ at all from a slave although he is owner of everything, but he is under guardians and managers until the date set by the father" (vv. 1–2). More than likely, this illustration is drawn from the ancient Roman laws that established the time of a son's maturity. In Roman society a son was not an adult until his father said he was. Furthermore, while legally a minor, a boy's "status was no different from that of a slave, even though he was the future owner of a vast estate. He could make no decisions; he had no freedom. On the other hand, at the time set by his father the child entered into his responsibility and freedom."[1] It was then that "the child was formally adopted by the father as his acknowledged son and heir."[2] This moving moment was coupled with great celebration.

B. The comparison. Likewise, before our acceptance into the family of God through faith, "we were children . . . held in bondage under the elemental things of the world" (v. 3). The phrase "elemental things" comes from the Greek word *stoicheia*. This term is used in Hebrews 5:12 to refer to the basic truths, or ABCs, of Christianity. In Galatians 4:3, however, the word has a different meaning. Here it designates the world's physical elements—things like the sun, moon, stars, and planets—which in Paul's day were thought to be controlled by gods and goddesses. Paul believed these false deities were demons (v. 8; compare 1 Cor. 8:4–6, 10:20; Eph. 6:12). Therefore, *stoicheia* in Galatians 4:3 probably refers to the demonic forces that temporarily control our world (John 12:31, 14:30). While we were unsaved, condemned by the Law, we were in bondage to evil spirits. The Law didn't enslave us to these powers, for God gave us the Law through His angels (Gal. 3:19). However, Satan used the Law to fulfill his own wicked schemes. John Stott captures this thought with characteristic clarity:

> Just as during a child's minority his guardian may ill-treat and even tyrannize him in ways which his father never intended, so the devil has exploited God's good law, in order to tyrannize men in ways God never intended. God intended the law to reveal sin and to drive men to Christ; Satan uses it to reveal sin and to drive men to despair. God meant the law as an interim step to man's justification; Satan uses it as the final step to his condemnation. God meant the

1. James Montgomery Boice, "Galatians," in *The Expositor's Bible Commentary,* 12 vols., ed. Frank E. Gaebelein (Grand Rapids, Mich.: Zondervan Publishing House, 1976), vol. 10, p. 471.

2. Boice, "Galatians," p. 471.

law to be a stepping-stone to liberty; Satan uses it as a cul-de-sac, deceiving his dupes into supposing that from its fearful bondage there is no escape.[3]

II. God's Action through His Son

Mercifully, the Lord stepped into history and defeated Satan's attempt to dominate us forever under the Law's curse.

A. The perfect time. God moved into our demon-ruled world "when the fulness of the time came" (4:4a). This occurred when the Roman government had established peace and built a road system that greatly aided travel; when most of the known world spoke one language—Greek; when the Greek and Roman mythical gods were losing their ability to satisfy the common people's spiritual hunger; when the Law of Moses had completed its work of preparing men and women, boys and girls, for the Savior and His message of grace.

B. The best way. At this perfect moment in history, God did two things.

1. **He sent His Son.** First, He "sent forth His Son, born of a woman, born under the Law" (v. 4b). The second person of the Trinity, the Son, was sent to earth by the heavenly Father to miraculously join with a sinless human nature in the womb of a sinful Jewish virgin named Mary. At that moment, the Son of God also became the Son of Man. This God-man, Jesus Christ, was subject to the Mosaic Law; yet unlike all who preceded Him and all who will follow, He met the Law's requirements perfectly. Consequently, Christ's divinity, humanity, and righteousness uniquely qualified Him to "redeem those who were under the Law" (v. 5a). As John Stott explains: "If He had not been man, He could not have redeemed men. If He had not been a righteous man, He could not have redeemed unrighteous men. And if He had not been God's Son, He could not have redeemed men for God or made them the sons of God."[4] Why did the Father send Christ to purchase us from the slave market of sin? Why did God sacrifice so much for souls as unworthy as us? So "that we might receive the adoption as sons" (v. 5b). Because He is merciful and loving, He desired to make us members of His everlasting family. By believing in His Son, we can become His spiritual sons.

2. **He sent His Spirit.** The second thing God did was "[send] forth the Spirit of His Son into our hearts, crying, 'Abba!

3. John R. W. Stott, *The Message of Galatians: Only One Way,* The Bible Speaks Today series (Downers Grove, Ill.: InterVarsity Press, 1968), p. 105.

4. Stott, *The Message of Galatians,* p. 106.

Father!'" (v. 6). When we become sons of God, the Father provides the Holy Spirit for us. We are never commanded to ask for the Spirit's indwelling presence—rather, we are given it at the moment we place our trust in Christ (compare Rom. 8:9–11, 14; Eph. 1:13–14, 4:30). If we are saved, the Spirit is at work in our lives, giving us the power we need to live the Christian life. And His presence within us seals and signifies our new familial relationship to God. We are now so close to the Lord that we can call Him Abba, or Daddy, the most intimate expression young Jewish children use of their fathers. "Therefore," Paul concludes, "you are no longer a slave, but a son; and if a son, then an heir through God" (Gal. 4:7). Once liberated by Christ through faith, we are given all the privileges and blessings that any other child of God has. That's grace!

A Challenge to Sons

Are you in God's family? If so, are you living like He wants His children to live? Are you bringing honor to His name? Just as we sometimes abuse our relationship with our earthly parents, we sometimes take unfair advantage of our standing before our heavenly Father. When we do step out of line, though, He doesn't always lower the boom. In fact, He frequently uses the Spirit to convict us of our wrongdoing so we'll seek forgiveness and continue to grow to spiritual maturity. But if we respond to the Spirit's promptings with an obstinate heart, the Lord will discipline us (Heb. 12:5–13). The choice is ours. Will you choose to obey your Father? He will always ask you to do what is best, and He will never fail to give you the strength to do it.

III. Paul's Appeal to Christians

With this groundwork laid, Paul exhorts the Galatian Christians to live as God's sons, not as Satan's slaves. "When you did not know God, you were slaves to those which by nature are no gods. But now that you have come to know God, or rather to be known by God, how is it that you turn back again to the weak and worthless [demonic spirits], to which you desire to be enslaved all over again?" (Gal. 4:8–9). If we don't belong to God, we belong to Satan. There's no middle ground, no other option. We may not have believed that Satan was our master in our non-Christian days, but that doesn't negate the fact that he was. While we were under Satan's control, the Lord sought us out. He pursued; we ran. He revealed Himself; we hid. He wooed us; we fought Him on every front . . . until He won us over. The Galatian believers knew that they had come to a God who loved them so much He wouldn't give up on them. They knew they did not *deserve* to be His children, yet they were acting as if they didn't *desire* to be in His family. How were they showing this? By keeping "days and months and seasons and years" (v. 10). They were worshiping on Saturdays rather than Sundays, thereby keeping the Jewish Sabbath. They were observing other Jewish celebrations, such as the Passover and the Feast of Tabernacles. In brief, they were striving to obey the calendar of events laid out in the Mosaic Law in order to secure their salvation. How tragic! They were already God's children, yet they were living as if they were orphans. Disheartened, Paul finally exclaims, "I fear for you, that perhaps I have labored over you in vain" (v. 11). If you have ever discipled someone who seems to be growing but eventually slips back into an unbiblical belief system and lifestyle, you can understand Paul's feelings toward the Galatian believers. What disappointment and frustration!

IV. Our Response to the Truth
This section of Paul's letter leaves us with at least two lessons to ponder.

A. The answer to spiritual bondage is redemption. If you are without Christ, you are under the dominion of Satan. The only way God can be your Master and Father is for you to accept His Son Jesus through faith alone. Leave the kingdom of darkness and enter the kingdom of light before death visits your door, removing your last chance to become a member of God's forever family.

B. The answer to legal bondage is discernment. If you're a believer, you'll undoubtedly come in contact with people who want to put you under a law of dos and don'ts. They will say that unless you keep these rules, God won't be pleased with you. In fact, they may add that the road to full justification and sanctification is through obedience to this legal code. Don't believe them! They may be sincere, well-meaning people, but they are wrong—dead wrong. Certainly, God wants us to keep His commands, and yes, they aid our growth in godliness and are an expression of our faith (John 14:15, 15:10–11; Phil. 2:12–13; James 2:14–26). But rule-keeping is not the way to righteousness either before or after conversion. Christ alone by faith alone is the only way to become right and stay right before God.

Living Insights

"No longer a slave, but a son" (Gal. 4:7a). What a proclamation! We can enjoy an intimacy with God which is best described by the word *Abba*. Let's delve into the vivid contrast portrayed in this passage.

- What does Scripture say about slavery? What about sonship? Locate a Bible concordance and look up the words *slave, servant, son, heir, born,* and *birth.* Record your observations in the space below. We think you'll quickly see the distinctions between these two positions.

Slave

Verse: _____ Observations: _____

_____

_____

Servant

Verse: _____ Observations: _____

_____

_____

Son

Verse: _____ Observations: _____

_____

_____

Heir

Verse: _____ Observations: _____

_____

_____

Born

Verse: _____ Observations: _____

_____

_____

Birth

Verse: _____ Observations: _____

_____

_____

Living Insights
Study Two ■■

Children of God . . . you and me. Have you thought about what this means, about our royal position as children of the King?

- Think in human terms for a minute. If your father were your country's king, how would your life be different? How do royal children live? List some of their privileges below. See the column titled "You"? As you read through the privileges of a royal child, place a check (√) by those you currently enjoy. Have you left some blank spaces? Put an asterisk (*) by one or two areas you want to enjoy and think about a plan for reaping these benefits. Close your time by having an audience with the King.

Royal Privileges	You

Solving the Pastor-People Conflict
Galatians 4:12–20

The night before Jesus was crucified, He prayed that all Christians would become as one, bonded together by love (John 13:34, 17:20–26). Why His stress on unity? Because it would be a sign to the non-Christian world that He was who He claimed to be—God's eternal Son. Christ staked His identity and mission on unity in the Church. If unbelievers fail to see this oneness, it is not surprising that they dismiss the validity of Christianity.

This is a sobering thought, especially when we realize the many times and ways Christians have lashed out at one another. Throughout history, believers have fought over doctrine, management practices, finances, ministerial philosophy, evangelistic approaches, Sunday school curriculum, hymnal purchases . . . the list goes on and on. Sometimes the disputes have been resolved in a spirit of forgiveness and compassion. Many times, however, conflicts have been aggravated by prideful individuals who were more intent on winning than resolving. This warlike approach leaves Christians scarred for decades and non-Christians out in the cold without a Savior.

So serious are these ramifications that Paul Billheimer has concluded: "Disunity in the Body of Christ is the scandal of the ages. The greatest sin of the Church is not lying, stealing, drunkenness, adultery—not even murder—but the sin of *disunity*."[1]

One of the greatest seedbeds for disunity in the Church is the relationship between a minister and his congregation. Too often, both parties end up with unfulfilled expectations and crushed feelings fertilized by misunderstandings and critical attitudes. This is not a new problem; churches have wrestled with it for centuries. In fact, Paul had to close up a deep rift that threatened to destroy the bond between himself and the Galatian church. By observing how he handled this conflict, we will learn how we should deal with pastor-people disagreements.

I. Misunderstandings about Paul
Like many pastors today, Paul was the victim of some false perceptions. Three of them are especially common in the contemporary Church.

A. He is not what he appears to be in his letters. This is the criticism of *hypocrisy*. Paul mentions it in 2 Corinthians and flatly contradicts it:

---

1. Paul E. Billheimer, *Love Covers: A Biblical Design for Unity in the Body of Christ* (Minneapolis, Minn.: Bethany House Publishers; Washington, Pa.: Christian Literature Crusade, 1981), p. 31.

For I do not wish to seem as if I would terrify you by my letters. For they say, "His letters are weighty and strong, but his personal presence is unimpressive, and his speech contemptible." Let such a person consider this, that what we are in word by letters when absent, such persons we are also in deed when present. (10:9-11)

B. He is not an apostle, though he claims to be. This charge challenges Paul's *authority*. And as we've seen in previous lessons, the Judaizers were using this fallacious assertion to undermine Paul's ministry in Galatia. But Paul undercuts their claim by demonstrating the genuineness of his apostleship (Gal. 1:1, 11-2:10).

C. He is not a warm, tender pastor but a cold, intimidating bully. Paul confronts this attack against his *personality* with words that convey a pastor's heart:

For we never came with flattering speech, as you know, nor with a pretext for greed—God is witness— nor did we seek glory from men, either from you or from others, even though as apostles of Christ we might have asserted our authority. But we proved to be gentle among you, as a nursing mother tenderly cares for her own children. Having thus a fond affection for you, we were well-pleased to impart to you not only the gospel of God but also our own lives, because you had become very dear to us. (1 Thess. 2:5-8)

Filling a Pastor's Shoes

Being a minister today is not easy—but the task becomes impossible when a pastor is straitjacketed by unrealistic, narrow-minded demands from his congregation.

If the pastor is young, they say he lacks experience; if his hair is gray, then he's too old for the young people.

If he has 5 or 6 children, he has too many; if he has no children, he's setting a bad example.

If he preaches from his notes, he has canned sermons and is dry; if his messages are extemporaneous, he is not deep.

If he is attentive to the poor people in the church, they claim he is playing to the grandstand; if he pays attention to the wealthy, he is trying to be an aristocrat.

If he uses too many illustrations, he neglects the Bible; if he doesn't use enough stories, he isn't clear.

If he condemns wrong, he's cranky; if he doesn't preach against sin, they say he's a compromiser.

If he preaches the truth, he's offensive; if he doesn't preach the truth, then he's a hypocrite.

If he fails to please everybody, he's hurting the church and ought to leave; if he does please everybody, he has no convictions.[2]

No wonder the attrition rate in the pastorate is so high. Who could ever satisfy people with demands like these? And if someone tried, how long would he last before becoming frustrated, cynical, burned-out, or unemployed? Pastors need our prayers and help, not our hidden agendas and unreasonable qualifications.

II. Paul's Approach to the Galatian Problem

In the first three chapters of his letter to the Galatians, Paul musters his historical and theological arsenal against the Judaizers' false gospel and their accusations of him. In chapter 4, his tone begins to change—he moves from defending to exhorting, from challenging to complimenting, from refuting to remembering. Paul the vigorous apologist becomes Paul the loving pastor. He pleads with the Galatian believers, his spiritual brethren and children (vv. 12a, 19a), to return to the truth they once embraced.

A. Paul's appeal. "I beg of you, brethren, become as I am, for I also have become as you are. You have done me no wrong" (v. 12). Paul gets on his knees and implores the Galatian Christians to become like him—free and satisfied in Christ (compare Acts 26:28–29). Why? Because when he first came to them, he didn't remain aloof but identified with them by adopting many of their Gentile customs (compare 1 Cor. 9:19–22). Furthermore, while he was with them, they didn't hassle him. They responded to his loving self-sacrifice in kind, leaving no room for bad memories in Paul's mind. Now, urges the apostle, it is the Galatians' turn to walk in his footsteps.

2. As quoted by Richard De Haan in *Men Sent from God* (Grand Rapids, Mich.: Radio Bible Class, 1966), pp. 5–6.

```
┌─ Setting an Example ──────────────────────────────┐
```
Setting an Example

We face two extremes in our churches today. One is distancing ourselves from non-Christians to such an extent that we never have any meaningful contact with them. The other is identifying so closely with unbelievers that we become virtually indistinguishable from them. The balance we need to seek is modeled by Paul. When with Jews, he adopted those Jewish customs not antithetical to Christianity in order to save as many Jews as he could (Acts 16:1–3, 18:18, 21:20–26; 1 Cor. 9:20). Likewise, when he spent time with Gentiles, he became as they in matters indifferent to Christianity so he might win them to the gospel (Gal. 2:11–21, 1 Cor. 9:21). In nonessentials, we need to lay our differences aside and make ourselves as palatable as possible to our unbelieving contacts.[3] By emulating Paul, we can bring many new citizens into Christ's eternal kingdom.

B. The Galatians' attitude. Paul reminisces, "You know that it was because of a bodily illness that I preached the gospel to you the first time" (Gal. 4:13). No one is sure what hampered Paul physically. Perhaps he contracted malaria while on the mosquito-infested coast of Pamphylia, just south of Galatia. Some think he had a painful eye disorder because of his remark that the Galatians would have given him their eyes if they could (v. 15; compare 6:11). Or maybe Paul is referring to the results of the stoning he survived during his evangelistic ministry in Lystra (Acts 14:19–20, 2 Tim. 3:11). Whatever the ailment, it was serious enough to cause him to come under the Galatians' care for an extended period. And care they did. They refused to "despise or loathe" Paul for being unable to meet their needs as a healthy pastor could (Gal. 4:14a). Instead, they welcomed him "as an angel of God, as Christ Jesus Himself" (v. 14b). They listened to Paul as if he were an angelic messenger sent from God. What respect and compassion they showed! But now, Paul laments, their attitude toward him has shifted. He asks, "Where then is that sense of blessing you had? For I bear witness, that if possible, you would have plucked out your eyes and given them to me. Have I therefore become your enemy by telling you the truth?" (vv. 15–16).

---

3. Some helpful sources on altering our lifestyles for the gospel's sake are listed in this study guide's final section, Books for Probing Further.

Speaking the Truth

The Galatians turned from treating Paul like an angel to looking on him as an enemy. Who changed? Not Paul—his message and method remained the same. But when he confronted the Galatians with their break from the true gospel, they turned on him, becoming defensive and despiteful. Christian unity was threatened because Paul had spoken the truth. How ironic! Yet the same problem arises today. Churches split, friendships shatter, pastors resign . . . frequently because someone has dared to tell the truth. It doesn't have to be this way. Truth can heal our relationships if we will take off our pride and clothe ourselves with humility, compassion, and tact. This approach will not ensure that conflicts will disappear, but it will bring honor to God and help facilitate reconciliation.

C. Paul's attitude. Turning his thoughts to the Judaizers who have duped the Galatian Christians, Paul says, "These heretical teachers go to great lengths to flatter you, but their motives are rotten. They want to shut you out of the free world of God's grace so that you will always depend on them for approval and direction, making them feel important" (v. 17).[4] Paul realizes that false teachers desire people to follow *them,* not Christ. And although the Judaizers were showering the Galatians with compliments—a practice Paul deems good when done with the right motives (v. 18)—these legalists were doing it to spotlight themselves and enslave the Galatians under the Law. With the tender heart of a pastor, Paul explains that his motive has always been to serve the Galatian believers until Christ was formed in them (v. 19). When we place our faith in Jesus, we are immediately indwelt by Him (Col. 1:27). But His presence does not automatically make us Christlike in character. That takes an entire lifetime. God's goal for us is that we grow into Christ's image (Rom. 8:29; Eph. 4:13, 15). Every biblical command and principle related to the Christian life has been given with this end in mind. Paul's plea to the believers in Galatia is that they conform themselves to Christ, not to the false teachers in their midst. The Galatians' shift away from a life marked by grace has left Paul completely baffled (Gal. 4:20).

---

4. This paraphrase is given by Eugene H. Peterson in his book *Traveling Light: Reflections on the Free Life* (Downers Grove, Ill.: InterVarsity Press, 1982), p. 126.

Imaging Christ

"What should matter to the people is not the pastor's appearance, but whether *Christ* is speaking through him. And what should matter to the pastor is not the people's favour, but whether *Christ* is formed in them. The church needs people who, in listening to their pastor, listen for the message of Christ, and pastors who, in labouring among the people, look for the image of Christ. Only when pastor and people thus keep their eyes on Christ will their mutual relations keep healthy, profitable and pleasing to almighty God."[5]

Are you seeking Christ, modeling your life after His by the power of the Holy Spirit? Are you declaring Christ, presenting Him as the only way to a right relationship with God? Are you working with your pastor, praying for him and helping him carry out the tasks of ministry? Are you listening to preachers who put Christ above all else? These searching questions demand honest answers. Survey your situation and examine your heart; see if you need to get your life back on track.

III. Becoming Part of the Solution

We've covered a good deal of ground in this lesson. But before we bring it to a close, let's consider two principles that can help us become unifiers rather than dividers.

A. Embrace the truth—no matter how much it may hurt. If you're the speaker, tell the truth. If you're the listener, welcome the truth. If you're the decision maker, seek the truth. Regardless of your position or role in your local church or community, be a lover and model of truth—even when the truth might wound you or someone else.

B. Watch your attitude—no matter how well you know another person. The first month or two of living or working with someone is usually a sort of honeymoon period. But as the months and years pass and knowledge of one another goes deeper, relationships can become strained. If attitudes aren't kept in check, weaknesses may begin to overshadow strengths. Remember, there will always be things we dislike in others, and there will always be things others dislike in us. Only genuine Christian love exuding from us all can bridge the gaps and bring unity to Christ's Church.

5. John R. W. Stott, *The Message of Galatians: Only One Way,* The Bible Speaks Today series (Downers Grove, Ill.: InterVarsity Press, 1968), p. 119.

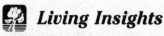 *Living Insights*

Conflict within the Body of Christ is as old as the Church itself. And while conflict is inevitable, there are steps we can take to diminish its effects.

- Paul deals with church relationships in his first letter to Timothy. Old, young, slaves, masters, widows, leaders, and false teachers are just some of the people he discusses. Read through 1 Timothy, and see if you can discover some principles for harmonious relationships between such diverse individuals. Record your findings in the chart below.

1 Timothy	
Verses	Principles for Harmonious Relationships

Living Insights

As our lesson unfolded, did you think about your relationship with your pastor? Is it characterized by harmony or conflict?

- Write a letter to your pastor. If your relationship is harmonious, thank him for the part he plays. Thank him for telling the truth and mention the special gifts you think he brings to the ministry. Encourage him. Perhaps, however, you're battling with your pastor. As you write to him, confront the issues. If he has offended you by telling you the truth, confess your feelings. Use this letter to bring restoration to the relationship. If you're a pastor, use your creativity to express appreciation to your sheep. You may even consider reading them your letter during a morning or evening worship service. What a way to encourage your church!

To Those Who Want to Be under the Law
Galatians 4:21–31

The vast array of religious beliefs is overwhelming, even to those who spend their lives studying them. It seems that no two religions have much in common. Take the concept of God, for example. In Judaism, God exists as one person; in Christianity, He is tripersonal—Father, Son, and Holy Spirit—yet one being; in Hinduism, God is personal and impersonal at the same time. Examples abound, but all illustrate the same truth: Each religion differs from every other in practically every fundamental belief. The variety seems endless and confusing[1]—except in one area.

All religions, with a single exception, teach that salvation involves human achievement. These religions may disagree on what man must do to be saved, but they all believe we must earn salvation in some way. Christianity stands apart from all other religions, proclaiming that God alone saves. Divine favor, says Christianity, cannot be earned—it can only be bestowed. We come before God like poverty-stricken beggars, with nothing to offer but our sinful selves. Out of His overflowing grace, God pours His riches upon us, providing complete forgiveness and everlasting life.

This difference between salvation by works and salvation by grace is all the difference in the world. A religion of works leads to slavery and death; a religion of grace brings freedom and life. Works-oriented people can't quite accept this truth. They think they can lift themselves out of the spiritual poorhouse if they just labor hard enough. In the last section of Galatians 4, Paul grants the validity of this position in order to refute it. With a master-stroke, he shows that a work-your-way-up religion causes its own downfall.

I. The Argument Analyzed

Paul's doctrinal case against the legalistic Judaizers is brought to a climax and a close in Galatians 4:21–31. Here he uses the Judaizers' method of argument and exegesis to disprove their position. He opens with a question (v. 21), provides some historical background from the life of Abraham (vv. 22–23), allegorizes the history given (vv. 24–27), and, finally, applies the allegory to the Galatians' situation (vv. 28–31). As we'll see, this is a fitting end to his vigorous defense of salvation by grace through faith alone.

A. The question.
"Tell me, you who want to be under law, do you not listen to the law?" (v. 21). The legalists, and the Christians who joined them, were not forced to live according to the Law.

1. A book that categorizes the many different religious perspectives into seven world views is *Perspectives: Understanding and Evaluating Today's World Views,* by Norman L. Geisler and William D. Watkins (San Bernardino, Calif.: Here's Life Publishers, 1984).

They made that choice freely; therefore, they were responsible for it. Focusing on their decision, Paul wants to know if they have really thought it through. Have they come to grips with the whole Law—Genesis through Deuteronomy—or have they just narrowed their sights to particular aspects of the Law? Paul's argument is built on the premise that the Judaizers and backslid Christians had adopted the regulations given to Moses while ignoring the promises made to Abraham. Consequently, their legalism was biblically unfounded.

Beginning Where People Are

This is not the first time Paul has built his case on grounds his opponents accept (compare 3:6–22). Throughout his ministry, Paul presents the gospel beginning where people are. With Jews, he turns to the Old Testament—their primary source of truth (Acts 17:1–3). With pagans, he uses their idols, poets, and prophets (vv. 22–23, 28; Titus 1:12). We, too, should seek common ground with unbelievers so we can gain a hearing for the good news about Christ. This involves listening to them, reading books they've written or read, spending leisure time with them . . . and above all, treating them as people for whom Christ died, not as enemies we need to defeat. Joseph Aldrich's thoughts on this issue hit close to home:

> Frequently the unsaved are viewed as enemies rather than victims of the Enemy. Spirituality is viewed as separation from the unsaved. The new Christian is told he has "nothing in common" with his unsaved associates. Quite frankly, I have a lot in common with them: a mortgage, car payments, kids who misbehave, a lawn to mow, a car to wash, a less-than-perfect marriage, a few too many pounds around my waist, and an interest in sports, hobbies, and other activities they enjoy. It is well to remember that Jesus was called a "friend of sinners." A *friend* of sinners.[2]

Are *you* a friend of the lost? Are you doing all you can to help them find new life? Remember, a good place to begin is where they are: their interests, their concerns, their beliefs.

2. Joseph C. Aldrich, *Life-style Evangelism: Crossing Traditional Boundaries to Reach the Unbelieving World* (Portland, Oreg.: Multnomah Press, 1981), p. 20.

B. The history. The Jews proudly boasted that they were descendants of Abraham. He was the father of their race. To him, God promised Canaan and a posterity greater in number than the stars of the sky and the sand of the seashore. Many Jews believed that their relationship to Abraham put them in proper standing before God. Because they were physical products of Abraham's seed, they thought they were heirs to God's promises and blessings. Paul wields the death blow to this belief by retelling the story of Abraham and the sons he had through Hagar and Sarah. Abraham had "one [son] by the bondwoman [Hagar] and one by the free woman [Sarah]. But the son by the bondwoman was born according to the flesh, and the son by the free woman through the promise" (Gal. 4:22–23). When God promised Abraham that he would have a son, Abraham was one hundred years old; Sarah was ninety and barren (Gen. 16:1, 17:15–17, 18:9–14). The only way they could have a child was by God performing a miracle. But they chose not to wait for the Lord; instead, Sarah convinced Abraham to have a child through Hagar, their maid (16:2–4). The result was Ishmael—a son conceived only by natural means, a son not of promise or grace but of sin and human effort. Later, however, the Lord fulfilled His promise to Abraham by miraculously enabling Sarah to have a son (21:1–3). When this infant was born, Abraham named him Isaac.

C. The allegory. Paul plumbs the depths of these historical facts and discovers a spiritual meaning that reveals the inherent fallacy of legalism.[3] The chart below brings out the many contrasts Paul discusses.[4]

A Religion of Works	The Religion of Grace
Hagar, the Bondwoman	Sarah, the Free Woman
Ishmael—Natural Birth	Isaac—Supernatural Birth
The Old Covenant	The New Covenant
Earthly Jerusalem	Heavenly Jerusalem
Legalistic Religion	Authentic Christianity

3. Paul's use of allegory is ably discussed by E. Earle Ellis in *Paul's Use of the Old Testament* (1957; reprint, Grand Rapids, Mich.: Baker Book House, 1981), and by Colin Brown in "Parable, Allegory, Proverb" in *The New International Dictionary of New Testament Theology,* 3 vols. (Grand Rapids, Mich.: Zondervan Publishing House, 1976), vol. 2, pp. 747–48, 754–56.

4. This chart is a modified version of one used in "Galatians" by James Montgomery Boice in *The Expositor's Bible Commentary,* 12 vols., ed. Frank E. Gaebelein (Grand Rapids, Mich.: Zondervan Publishing House, 1976), vol. 10, p. 483.

Hagar and Sarah represent two covenants. "A covenant is a solemn agreement between God and men, by which He makes them His people and promises to be their God."[5] Hagar represents the old covenant delivered to Moses on Mount Sinai. This agreement bound the Jews—citizens of the earthly Jerusalem—to the Law's statutes, sacrifices, and punishments (Gal. 4:24–25). The new covenant, symbolized by Sarah, is based on God's promises, not His Law. This agreement was ratified by Christ on Calvary; He sealed it with His own blood (compare Heb. 9:11–28). All who come to God by faith alone enter into this covenant, thereby becoming spiritual children of Abraham and citizens of the heavenly Jerusalem (Gal. 4:26–27). Paul's point in this allegory is brought out by James Boice:

> On the most superficial level, Isaac and Ishmael were alike in that both were sons of Abraham. But on a more fundamental level they were entirely different. In the same way, Paul argues, it is not enough merely to claim Abraham as one's father. Both Christians and Jews did that. The question is: Who is our mother and in what way were we born? If Hagar is our mother, then we were born of purely human means and are still slaves. If our mother is Sarah, then the birth was by promise, and we are free men.[6]

D. The application. To the believers in Galatia, Paul says, "You brethren, like Isaac, are children of promise" (v. 28). When we place our trust in Christ alone, we, too, become related to Abraham and Sarah in the only way that makes any spiritual difference. We are born supernaturally into God's family and made everlasting heirs of heaven's imperishable riches. But until we enter heaven's gate, *we must first expect to be persecuted by our half brothers*—religious people who claim to be part of Christ's Church but are not. Just as Ishmael ridiculed and scorned Isaac (Gen. 21:8–9), so legalists will persecute believers (Gal. 4:29). It has been this way throughout history. Jesus was opposed, mocked, and condemned by the religious leaders of His day. The Judaizers tried to make life a living hell for Paul. Protestant groups in the late Middle Ages and Reformation were brutalized by the papacy and loyal Catholic orders. In our day, Christians are still snubbed, arrested, beaten, and even killed by supposedly loyal followers of Christ. When law-keeping and grace-living clash, we can't expect much else. This leads to a

5. John R. W. Stott, *The Message of Galatians: Only One Way,* The Bible Speaks Today series (Downers Grove, Ill.: InterVarsity Press, 1968), p. 124.

6. Boice, "Galatians," p. 484.

second point: *we must recognize the absolute incompatibility of man-made religion and God's provision.* Hagar and Ishmael symbolize man's attempt to achieve what only God can do. This humanistic approach to the Lord cannot coexist with the way of faith; therefore, just as Hagar and Ishmael were cast out of Abraham's household (Gen. 21:10, 12), so must works-oriented religions and beliefs be removed from God's household (Gal. 4:30). "[Christians] are not children of a bondwoman, but of the free woman" (v. 31).

II. Our Response: Law or Grace

Paul's argument leaves us with two lingering thoughts we should seriously ponder.

A. When it comes to law and grace, we have to get off the fence. We cannot fluctuate between rules and faith, mixing them in our approach to God. He will not allow that. Either we come to Him His way, or we do not come at all. C. S. Lewis once wrote: "There are only two kinds of people in the end: those who say to God, 'Thy will be done,' and those to whom God says, in the end, *'Thy* will be done.'" [7] The former are people of faith and citizens of heaven; the latter are people of works and slaves of hell. Until we trust in Christ alone, we all belong to the second group. Where is your membership?

B. Once we stop fence-straddling, we will realize how incompatible law and grace really are. The free life can't survive the structured demands of rule-centered living. Conversely, law-keeping can't maintain a grip on a truly liberated life. As Christians, we are called to a life of freedom. Let's start living it—today.

 Living Insights

Study One

This particular portion of Galatians centers on the allegory of Hagar and Sarah. Let's dig deeper into this passage to understand Paul's argument more fully.

- Reread the actual accounts about the births of Ishmael and Isaac. Focus your attention on Genesis 16 for insights into Hagar and Ishmael; then turn to Genesis 21 to study Sarah and Isaac. Look for points of contrast in the two chapters. Record your observations in the space provided.

---

7. C. S. Lewis, *The Great Divorce* (New York, N.Y.: Macmillan Publishing Co., 1946), p. 72.

Hagar and Ishmael—Genesis 16

Observations: _____

_____

_____

_____

_____

_____

_____

_____

_____

_____

_____

Sarah and Isaac—Genesis 21

Observations: _____

_____

_____

_____

_____

_____

_____

_____

_____

_____

_____

_____

_____

Continued on next page

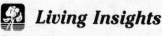 *Living Insights*

Gather a group of good friends or family to discuss some implications of this lesson. Encourage all present to participate in the discussion—everyone's thoughts are worth hearing. If you are studying on your own, use this time for personal reflection.

- The application of Galatians 4:29 is clear: we must expect persecution. Why? Do you agree that persecution comes from "half brothers"—those who claim to be part of God's family? Share some real-life situations when you have been persecuted because of your faith.
- How do people try to unite man-made religion with God's provision? Share any observations you have made. Do you recognize that these two categories are absolutely incompatible? If so, how did you come to this discovery?
- Conclude the discussion by asking each person to share a truth they have learned thus far from Galatians. Remember some key words: *liberty, the gospel, affirming, hypocrisy, backsliding, legalism, the Law, the tutor, slavery, sonship, confrontation.*

Freedom, Faith, Love, and Truth

Galatians 5:1–12

Picture yourself as an impoverished prospector, tirelessly searching for fortune on your small farm in South Africa during the 1930s. After a heavy storm, you walk up and down your land to see if the rain washed up anything. Eventually, you come across an unusual stone the size of a hen's egg. As you wipe the mud from its surface, it begins to look like a diamond in the rough. Trembling with excitement, you rush home to show the stone to your family. A few days later you sell the "rock"—a 726-carat diamond—for $315,000. Sound incredible? Yes, but it actually happened to a poor prospector named Jacobus Jonker.[1]

What if this had really happened to you? Would you do everything you could to protect that stone? You bet you would! You'd probably lock it in the most secure vault you could find.

But what if you found something even more precious than a huge diamond? Suppose you discovered the priceless gift of liberty in Christ. Through Him, you realized you could be free—really free. So you reached out your empty hands and received the precious gem. Would you guard your newfound treasure? Would you do all you could to keep thieves from taking it away?

The Galatian Christians did have this jewel, yet they allowed legalists to break into their lives and rob them. Shocked, Paul sped off a letter to the Galatians, defending the free life and urging them to take back what was rightfully theirs. In chapter 5 of this letter, he continues his appeal with some of the strongest language we've seen from him.

I. A Statement of Our Liberty

Galatians 5 opens with a declaration of our liberty in Christ and a command we should obey as a result.

A. The declaration. "It was for freedom that Christ set us free" (v. 1a). Jesus died for us on the cross so that through faith in Him, we could live as free people. He has liberated us from the penalty and guilt of sin, divine wrath, satanic domination, the Law's curse, and the fear of ultimate judgment. And He has freed us to enjoy a new kind of life—one in which we can live by the Spirit's power, joyfully obey God, love and serve others, come immediately into the Lord's presence through prayer, and grow in our walk with God. We have the gem of promise. We didn't pay anything for it; Christ paid for it in full.

---

1. See *Diamonds Eternal,* by Victor Argenzio (New York, N.Y.: David McKay Co., 1974), pp. 50–52.

B. The command. "Therefore," Paul says, "keep standing firm and do not be subject again to a yoke of slavery" (v. 1b). God never commands us to submit to everyone regardless of who they are or what they say and do. We are called to exercise wisdom—to discern between truth and error, right and wrong, and the genuine article as opposed to a fake (Matt. 7:15–23, 10:16, 24:23–26; Heb. 5:14; 1 John 4:1–6). So when people tell us we need to follow their works-centered plan to become acceptable to God, we must "contend earnestly for the faith" (Jude 3) and flatly refuse to give up our priceless gift of freedom.

II. Consequences for Those Who Embrace Legalism

But what if we allow a break-in, losing our liberty to legalism? Paul spells out four consequences that would befall us.

A. Christ will have no value. When we adopt legalism, we are saying that Jesus' sacrifice on the cross is insufficient to save us. We must add something to His payment in order to cancel our debt to God. We might as well set ourselves up as gods. Accepting legalism is rejecting the Savior. And if we turn against Him, His death will not benefit us at all (Gal. 5:2).

B. We will have to keep the whole Law. When we move from grace to works, we place ourselves back under the entire Mosaic Law. We cannot pick and choose which regulations we wish to obey; we would be obligated to obey them all (v. 3). And since it has already been established that we are lawbreakers, we would fall once again under the Law's curse (3:10–12, 22).

C. We will be alienated from Christ. God cannot accept us on the basis of works. Even our best deeds are like filthy rags in His sight (Isa. 64:6). So if we come to Him bringing good deeds that are dripping with mud, we are spurning His Son and will be cut off from Him, separated from the freedom we once enjoyed (Gal. 5:4a).

A Needed Clarification

Paul is not saying that believers can lose their salvation. Once we accept the gift of Christ, we are eternally secure in God's love (Rom. 8:35–39). However, if we try to *earn* God's favor after we are saved by faith, we are saying to Him, "We want You to treat us not as adopted sons but as lowly slaves. We'll try to earn Your family name by serving You." In responding this way, we hinder the transforming work of the Spirit and stunt our spiritual growth. So Paul's warning to believers is this: You will not mature in Christ if you try to earn His favor. Are you stunting your growth?

D. We will abandon the way of grace. Legalism and grace are two paths that never cross on the way to salvation. In fact, legalism leads to a dead end; only grace leads to God. By taking the way of works, we forsake the footpath of faith.

III. Contrasts between the Flesh and Faith

What are some differences between living in the flesh and living by faith? First, when we approach God on our own merit, we must work hard to earn our righteousness. But when we come to Him by faith, we can wait for the fulfillment of our righteousness—final glorification in heaven (Gal. 5:5; compare Rom. 8:30, 1 Cor. 15:42–44, 2 Cor. 4:17). Then, based upon Christ's work, we will be made pure and perfect. Think of it—no more handicaps, illnesses, sins, sorrows, temptations, or trials. We will be as good as we can possibly be and happier than we can ever imagine. Our own efforts could never achieve this glorious end. Another contrast between living in the flesh or by faith is given in Galatians 5:6: "In Christ Jesus neither circumcision nor uncircumcision means anything, but faith working through love." The essential factor in a flesh-oriented life is works; in a Christ-centered life, it is faith. And not just an intellectual faith but a practical one that is expressed in genuine, self-denying love for others (James 1:27, 2:14–17).

IV. Questions for Those Who Have "Fallen from Grace"

Paul's intense love for even fallen believers shines in Galatians 5:7–12. Here he expresses belief in them and comes down hard on those who have led the Galatians astray.

A. Who tripped you up? Paul acknowledges that the Galatian Christians had been "running well," combining their acceptance of divine grace with a life of responsible freedom (v. 7a). But someone had cut in on their stride, causing them to stumble in their obedience to the truth (v. 7b). Bruised and battered, they were leaving the track and strapping the weight of the Law around their ankles and chests. Now their mouths were turned down, and only grunts and groans could be heard where joy and hope once filled the air.

B. What effect is legalism having? Paul reminds these believers that God would not have hindered them in this way. The Lord had given them a radically new life; He had not let them run freely in order to trip them up and burden them down (v. 8). This obstacle had come from another source—one whose contaminating work had spread throughout the whole church, slowly but surely (v. 9). That's how it is with legalism. If you give in even a little, it will eventually permeate every facet of your life and ruin you.

C. Where will legalism lead? Paul is confident that the Galatian Christians will realize their error, shed the Law, and return to the free life (v. 10a). "But," he adds, "the one who is disturbing you shall bear his judgment, whoever he is" (v. 10b). God does not treat false teachers lightly. Indeed, since He holds those who teach more accountable than those who don't (James 3:1), we can be sure that teachers who mislead God's people will be judged severely if they don't repent (compare Matt. 18:5–9, Gal. 1:8–9).

D. Why am I still persecuted? The legalists claimed that Paul was in their camp on the issue of circumcision. Perhaps they pointed to the time when Paul circumcised Timothy (Acts 16:1–3).[2] At any rate, they tried to convince the Galatian believers that Paul did teach a faith-plus-works salvation. Paul wields a decisive blow to their claim: "If I still preach circumcision, why am I still persecuted? Then the stumbling block of the cross has been abolished" (Gal. 5:11). The gospel of grace is naturally offensive to people. Their pride leads them to believe that they can work their way in to heaven. And those who assure them that this is true receive their blessings. But if you puncture their pride by telling them that they must depend on Christ's work alone for salvation, they'll lash out with a vengeance. The very fact that Paul was suffering at the hands of the legalists proves that he was not in their camp. To make this clearer, Paul states, "Would that those who are troubling you would even mutilate themselves" (v. 12). He wishes the legalists' knives would slip, resulting in their castration. His remark sounds harsh and malicious to us, but as John Stott remarks: "We may be quite sure ... that it was due neither to an intemperate spirit, nor to a thirst for revenge, but to his deep love for the people of God and gospel of God. I venture to say that if we were as concerned for God's church and God's Word as Paul was, we too would wish that false teachers might cease from the land."[3]

---

2. Concerning this incident, expositor Stanley D. Toussaint writes: "Because of Timothy's good reputation (Acts 16:2) Paul wanted to take him along on the journey. . . . There was a problem, however. The Jews to whom Paul would be preaching the gospel would be offended if a man with a Jewish mother was uncircumcised. So Timothy was circumcised. . . . This appears to contradict Paul's thinking in Galatians 2:3–5 where he refused to let Titus be circumcised. The situations, however, were different. In Galatians 2 the issue was the method of justification; here [in Acts 16] it was a question of not giving offense (cf. 1 Cor. 9:19–23). The Jerusalem Council, of course, had determined circumcision was not necessary for salvation (Acts 15:10–11, 19). In Acts 16 Paul acted as he did for the sake of the ministry; it was a wise move." "Acts," in *The Bible Knowledge Commentary: New Testament Edition,* ed. John F. Walvoord and Roy B. Zuck (Wheaton, Ill.: Victor Books, 1983), p. 398.

3. John R. W. Stott, *The Message of Galatians: Only One Way,* The Bible Speaks Today series (Downers Grove, Ill.: InterVarsity Press, 1968), p. 136.

V. Questions Worth Asking Today

Paul's language is strong; his arguments, powerful. He rightly sees that the diamond of freedom is worth protecting. But we dare not just lock it in a vault and guard it. "Each day we must take up the stance of freedom again. If we fail to stand deliberately and consciously, the freedom will be lost."[4] Let's ask ourselves some questions that can guide us toward retaining and exercising our Christian liberty.

A. How highly do I value my freedom in Christ? Is it more precious to me than my money, home, family, friends, job, or reputation? If not, why?

B. How strongly do I resist having my freedom stolen? Do I submit to rules that strap me down spiritually, stopping or even reversing my Christian growth? If so, why? What can I do to regain my liberty?

C. How tolerant am I of other Christians and their exercise of freedom? Do I insist that fellow believers adopt my use of freedom? Or do I allow them the opportunity to express their liberty within the wider boundaries of Scripture?

D. How fully do I enjoy the benefits of my freedom? Do I derive satisfaction from serving God and others freely rather than under compulsion? Am I happy to finally have the resources to see and explore God's creation as never before?

 Living Insights

Study One

What you have in Christ is so much more valuable than a diamond—there aren't words to describe it adequately! This passage of Galatians gloriously radiates the message of liberty, a facet of the jewel we possess.

● Galatians 5:1–12 merits deeper digging. Jot down a reference that speaks on the same subject, and restate the words or phrases listed below.

Galatians 5:1–12

Verse 1: "freedom"

Cross-reference: _____   Restatement: _____

_____

---

4. Eugene H. Peterson, *Traveling Light: Reflections on the Free Life* (Downers Grove, Ill.: InterVarsity Press, 1982), p. 145.

Verse 1: "keep standing firm"

Cross-reference: _____ Restatement: _____

Verse 1: "yoke of slavery"

Cross-reference: _____ Restatement: _____

Verse 2: "circumcision"

Cross-reference: _____ Restatement: _____

Verse 3: "keep the whole Law"

Cross-reference: _____ Restatement: _____

Verse 4: "severed from Christ"

Cross-reference: _____ Restatement: _____

Verse 4: "fallen from grace"

Cross-reference: _____ Restatement: _____

Verse 6: "faith working through love"

Cross-reference: _____ Restatement: _____

Verse 7: "running well"

Cross-reference: _____ Restatement: _____

Verse 7: "hindered you"

Cross-reference: _____ Restatement: _____

Verse 9: "a little leaven leavens the whole lump"

Cross-reference: _____ Restatement: _____

_____

Verse 10: "disturbing you"

Cross-reference: _____ Restatement: _____

_____

Verse 11: "stumbling block of the cross"

Cross-reference: _____ Restatement: _____

_____

Verse 12: "mutilate themselves"

Cross-reference: _____ Restatement: _____

_____

Living Insights

Study Two

Once again, legalism rears its ugly head, and we see a warning given to those who embrace this rigid system. We must remember that freedom in Christ is a treasure to be highly valued, not a trinket to be tossed away. Legalism often creeps into a lifestyle at the expense of a God-given gift—enjoyment! Let's talk about the fun in your life.

- Do you have fun? _____ If so, how? _____

_____

_____

- Does your Christianity enhance your fun or does it put a damper on things?

_____

_____

_____

Continued on next page

- Can having fun be taken too far? _____ If so, how? _____

  _____

  _____

- How would you describe your ability to have fun: is it too easy, too hard, or just right? Expand on your answer.

  _____

  _____

  _____

- Have you ever prayed about fun? _____ Spend some time now talking about it with God.

Limiting Liberty with Love

Galatians 5:13–15, Romans 14:13–23

The minister had heard the story so many times that listening to it again evoked a strange mixture of anger and despair. Although the names, dates, and places had changed, the story's theme remained the same: one of his parishioners, Phil, had caused another Christian to stumble. This time, the casualty was Lana, a nineteen-year-old whom Phil had dated for the past seven months.

According to her parents, Phil had wooed Lana to her first taste of beer and wine, her first drug high, her first X-rated movie, and her first all-night date. His natural charm and live-and-let-live spirit attracted her like a moth to a flame. And though she struggled with his flippant attitude toward their church's moral teaching, she was captivated by his interpretation of Christian liberty. As he was fond of saying, "Jesus set us free so we could explore life to its fullest, not so we could be held back by someone's list of dos and don'ts." Persuaded by Phil, Lana spread her moral wings and flew into taboo airspace. There she joined a new flock of friends, saw new landscapes, and experienced new thrills. It all seemed so right, so liberating—at least for a while.

After five months the pleasures became oppressive demands; the scenery turned ugly and treacherous; and the once-inviting, eaglelike friends showed themselves to be disgusting vultures. Lana felt the current of her lifestyle pulling her down to the point of no return, but regardless of how hard she fought, she couldn't stop falling. Alcoholism, drug addiction, and sexual escapades held her in a death grip. Desperate, she finally turned to the two people who had repeatedly proved their love—her mother and father. Through an unbroken stream of tears, she bared her soul, pleading for help. Her parents, in turn, went to their pastor seeking solace and counsel.

As the minister listened to Lana's parents, he recalled his many confrontations with Phil. Each time he had explained to Phil that his concept of Christian freedom was unbiblical and damaging to himself and others. But each time Phil had stood his ground, refusing to even entertain the idea that he was wrong. How could Phil be stopped? What would convince him? The minister wasn't sure, but one thing was clear: Lana and her parents had become victims of freedom abuse. And, like anyone who is abused, they needed the warm embrace of love, not the cold finger of condemnation.

Do you know a Lana? Have you come under the spell of a Phil? Do you really understand what Lana learned the hard way—that authentic Christian freedom has limits? Or have you sided with Phil by rejecting this truth? These serious questions demand soul-searching answers. And only God's

Word provides a standard by which you can accurately gauge your responses. So let's turn to its pages before responding to these questions.

I. Clarification of Our Calling

Galatians 5:13 begins, "For you were called to freedom, brethren." These few words declare that all of us who have accepted Christ by faith are free. We have been liberated from the penalty of sin, the power of Satan, the wrath of God, and an accusing conscience. Now we are free to serve the Lord and become like His Son. But are we also free to disobey God and become self-centered? Are we free to sin as an expression of our new life in Christ? Absolutely not! In fact, the idea is absurd. It supposes that evil can be good, that wrong can be right. This kind of pseudofreedom actually enslaves rather than liberates. It shackles us to our pride, which says, "I want my way, and I won't let anyone or anything stop me from getting it."

II. Limitations on Our Liberty

True Christian freedom involves restraints—restraints that help, not hinder, our spiritual growth and service. Three limitations are given in Galatians 5:13–15.

A. We are not free to indulge the flesh. Paul states this limitation in these words: "Only do not turn your freedom into an opportunity for the flesh" (v. 13b). By the term *flesh*, Paul does not mean our physical bodies or the skin stretched over our bones and muscles. Rather, he is referring to our fallen nature—that propensity to sin we have within us our entire earthly lives. We must not allow our sinful nature to use our newfound freedom as a base of operations.[1] Our fallen nature was nailed to the cross when we trusted in Christ for our salvation (v. 24). Therefore, we should leave it there to die, not try to remove the nails and allow it to control us again. Who controls your life? Is it Christ or your flesh? Are you bowing before Him or self? You cannot serve both, and you will find real freedom only through obeying Christ (Mark 8:34–35, John 8:31–36, 1 Pet. 2:16–17). Remember, Christian freedom is freedom *from* sin to serve the Lord, not freedom *to* sin to serve self.

B. We are not free to exploit others. Using people to get what we want is an act of the flesh, not of faith. And when we treat others as things, we run the risk of hurting not only them but also ourselves (Gal. 5:15). Christian liberty urges us to go a different way. It beckons us to serve one another "through love" (v. 13b). This isn't a wishy-washy kind of love based on feelings.

1. This idea comes from the Greek term for *opportunity*, which means "a starting point or base of operations for an expedition." See James Montgomery Boice's commentary "Galatians" in *The Expositor's Bible Commentary*, 12 vols., ed. Frank E. Gaebelein (Grand Rapids, Mich.: Zondervan Publishing House, 1976), vol. 10, p. 493.

Nor is it the sort of love that says, "I'll meet you halfway." The love Paul speaks about is the love Christ manifested when He took our punishment upon Himself so we could escape God's wrath and enjoy His grace. This is *agapē* love—sacrificial love. It gives and gives and keeps on giving, even when it receives nothing in return. Do you have this kind of love for people? Do you reach out to those around you who cannot pay back your kindnesses or may be difficult to handle? Remember, Christian freedom treats people as persons to be served and loved, not as things to be used and abused.

C. We are not free to disregard the needs of others. The live-and-let-live philosophy of today is foreign to the Christian view of loving freedom. We are our brothers' keepers, and we are called to use our freedom to love others as we love ourselves (v. 14). Regarding this imperative, Eugene Peterson observes:

> To love my neighbors as less than myself is to treat them as a means to my ends. To love them as more would set them up for using me as a means to their ends. One way is as much a violation of love as the other, and as destructive of freedom. The command protects my freedom as much as yours. . . . No one sacrifices freedom at the expense of the other. All become increasingly free.[2]

Do you care for others' needs as much as your own? Are you willing to give up some comforts in order to make life better for someone else? Remember, Christian freedom was given for us to share liberally, not to possess greedily.

III. Guidelines for Our Balance

Realizing that genuine freedom comes with certain limits is important, but by itself this knowledge is not enough. We also need to know when we should restrain a *permissible* exercise of our liberty. We are not equally mature in our faith. Some of us can engage in various activities permitted by Scripture, while others still struggle with the acceptability of those practices. Of course, Phil had clearly stepped over the boundary and into sin. But there are times when we must also apply the brakes to the full exercise of our freedom. How will we know when to do this? Romans 14 gives some guidelines that will help us make this decision. This chapter's historical context involves meat from pagan animal sacrifices. Christians were divided over whether it was right to buy and eat this meat, so Paul addresses their disagreement. He points out that nothing in God's creation is evil in itself, but because some people don't accept this fact, they

2. Eugene H. Peterson, *Traveling Light: Reflections on the Free Life* (Downers Grove, Ill.: Inter-Varsity Press, 1982), p. 155.

falter in their faith when they see fellow Christians eating "unclean" foods (vv. 13–14).[3] Consequently, Paul says, believers need to temper their freedom with love. He conveys this counsel through three timeless principles.

A. **When our liberty could hurt a fellow Christian, we should yield.** As Paul states, "If because of food your brother is hurt, you are no longer walking according to love. Do not destroy with your food him for whom Christ died" (v. 15). Helping fellow believers grow in their faith is far more important than exercising our freedom to its fullest. Indeed, Christ set us free so we could use our freedom to serve, not destroy. So whenever we think our actions may hinder another Christian's walk with God, we should restrain ourselves. Because you are free, do you flaunt the fact no matter what? Or do you hold back when love says you must?

B. **When our liberty could hinder God's work, we should yield.** "Do not," Paul writes, "let what is for you a good thing be spoken of as evil; for the kingdom of God is not eating and drinking, but righteousness and peace and joy in the Holy Spirit" (vv. 16–17). Godly living and Christian unity are the sum and substance of God's spiritual kingdom. When we use our freedom in a way that hampers holiness or harmony, we impede the development of His kingdom. Are you frustrating the efforts of the King to further His spiritual dominion? Or are you pressing your freedom into His service, using it to conquer more territory for Him?

C. **When our liberty creates unrest in our consciences, we should yield.** "The faith which you have, have as your own conviction before God. Happy is he who does not condemn himself in what he approves. But he who doubts is condemned if he eats, because his eating is not from faith; and whatever is not from faith is sin" (vv. 22–23). When we feel uneasy about the morality of a certain practice, we should not do it. The internal unrest may be the Holy Spirit telling us that for us the action is wrong. Do you practice something you think may not be right? Or do you allow your conscience to guide you in one direction until you are convinced on biblical grounds that you should redirect your steps?

Liberty, Love, and You

Remember the story about Lana and Phil? With whom do you identify? Are you like Phil, a freedom abuser, or like

---

3. This issue is more completely discussed in the study guide *Relating to Others in Love: A Study of Romans 12–16*, ed. Bill Watkins, from the Bible-teaching ministry of Charles R. Swindoll (Fullerton, Calif.: Insight for Living, 1985), pp. 34–41.

Lana, a freedom loser, or like her pastor, a freedom protector? If you're a freedom abuser, you need to slam on the brakes and turn your life back to traveling God's way. If you're a freedom loser, you, too, need to apply the brakes and steer your life away from those who have led you astray. If you're a freedom protector, keep driving forward! We need more people like you to help the rest of us stay on the right road.

 Living Insights

Study One ▀▀▀▀▀▀▀▀▀▀▀▀▀▀▀▀▀▀▀▀▀▀▀▀▀▀▀▀▀▀▀▀▀▀▀▀▀

Christianity is not bondage—it is freedom. Yet we can misuse this freedom. For the sake of others, we must learn how to restrain our liberty.

- Let's personalize this lesson on liberty. Read the following four passages and write them out in your own words. As you paraphrase, think of how these verses apply to your expression of freedom.

Romans 14:13–21

_____

_____

_____

_____

_____

_____

_____

_____

_____

_____

_____

_____

_____

_____

Continued on next page

1 Corinthians 9:19–23

_____

_____

_____

_____

Galatians 5:13–15

_____

_____

_____

1 Peter 2:16–17

_____

_____

_____

📖 Living Insights

Study Two

Let's center our thoughts on the last three points in this lesson. The only person who knows how these principles affect your life is *you*.

- Think through each one of these guidelines carefully and determine what God would have you learn. Remember, only you can decide how they best apply in your life, so don't neglect the proper response as you jot down your thoughts.

1. When our liberty could hurt a fellow Christian, we should yield.

_____

_____

_____

2. When our liberty could hinder God's work, we should yield.

_____

_____

_____

_____

3. When our liberty creates unrest in our consciences, we should yield.

_____

_____

_____

Learning How to Walk

Galatians 5:16–25

She stood on a small platform towering high above the crowd. Several yards across from her was another tiny stage cloaked partially in darkness. Between her and that distant platform loomed an intimidating abyss and a long, silver strand seemingly leading nowhere. Her face was hot from the glare of the spotlight; her hands were clammy from fear. She offered a bow of confidence to the silhouettes below, then stood erect and faced the wire with her heart racing. She closed her eyes and looked deep into her soul, finding strength and determination that seemed to flow from an outside source. Still longing to remain safe, she slowly filled and emptied her lungs . . . and gazed at the wire stretched out in front of her.

Then she did it—she carefully stepped onto the wire, first with one foot, then the other. Soon she was halfway across, suspended in space and feeling as if she were free to spread her arms and take flight. But the ever present danger on every side made her yearn for the security of the metal platform. Finally reaching her destination, she quickly bowed to the applause from below and breathed a deep sigh of relief.

Like the circus's high-wire performer, Christians are perched on a tightrope, trying to avoid two extremes—legalism and licentiousness. Legalism presents itself as a platform of safety, saying "Stop taking the risks of the free life and come back to me." Licentiousness, on the other hand, beckons us to stretch out our arms and fly toward our basest desires in total self-abandonment. But God calls on us to keep walking the high wire of Christian freedom, balanced between playing it safe and living carelessly. What He is asking sometimes seems scary and impossible. Paul, however, reassures us that our walk can be filled with internal peace if we will only let the Holy Spirit help us.

I. The Issue Exposed

In our study of Galatians, we have seen that accepting Christ by faith alone liberates us from the Law's demands. That's why we can turn our backs on legalism and embark on the free life. But what can restrain us from using our freedom to plummet to the depths of immorality? We all feel the tug to step off the high wire and abuse our freedom. And yet, at the same time, our salvation has given us a new desire to put God's wishes ahead of our own. What is this inner conflict? Can it be resolved? If so, how? Our very balance depends on the answers to these questions.

II. The Problem Resolved

Paul gives us the answers we need in Galatians 5:16–25. He describes the tug-of-war within us and the opposing forces involved. Then he explains how we can achieve victory and maintain our balance.

A. The conflict within. Christians are human battlegrounds. Raging inside us is a war between our sinful nature and the Holy Spirit. "For the flesh sets its desire against the Spirit, and the Spirit against the flesh; for these are in opposition to one another" (v. 17a). Justification does not kill our depravity; it merely sets us free from the penalty of our fallen condition. Once we are saved, we enter a war we never had to face as unbelievers. We become embroiled in a fierce battle between the Spirit and the flesh, the new man and the old man. And until we die or Christ physically removes us from the earth, we will continue to experience this tumultuous warfare. Our every emotion, thought, choice, and act will feel the pressures caused by these two forces (v. 17b).

B. The forces described. To help us understand the powers warring within, Paul describes some of their results.

1. **"The deeds of the flesh."** These acts can be divided into four categories, each exposing the ugliness of our dark side. The first category is sexual; it includes "immorality, impurity, [and] sensuality" (v. 19). These sins cover all sexual offenses, whether public or private, between the married or the unmarried, or between homosexuals or bisexuals. The second division is religious, which includes "idolatry [and] sorcery" (v. 20a). Idolatry is the worship of anything other than God. False gods can be power, prestige, money, or self. Sorcery is " 'the secret tampering with the powers of evil,' "[1] an ancient equivalent to today's use of drugs to achieve "religious" experiences. The third category concerns personal relationships. "Enmities, strife, jealousy, outbursts of anger, disputes, dissensions, factions, [and] envying" are all signs of the flesh at work (vv. 20–21a). The last realm concerns excessive alcohol consumption. The sins here are obvious: "drunkenness [and] carousing" (v. 21a). All the deeds in these categories are simply examples of how far Christians can fall when they serve the flesh rather than the Spirit.

Clarifying a Warning

Paul holds up a warning sign when he tells us "that those who practice such [fleshly] things shall not inherit the kingdom of God" (v. 21b). This verse sounds as if believers can lose their salvation, but it means nothing of the sort. The interpretive key lies in the tense of the Greek term translated *practice.* The tense is present, indicating "a habitual continuation in fleshly

---

1. John R. W. Stott, *The Message of Galatians: Only One Way,* The Bible Speaks Today series (Downers Grove, Ill.: InterVarsity Press, 1968), p. 147.

sins rather than an isolated lapse."[2] Paul's point is that continual trafficking in sin is evidence of a lack of spiritual life, whereas occasional lapses into sin are a sign of carnality in the saved. Do you exhibit one of these lifestyles? If the former, you probably still need salvation; if the latter, you need to surrender entirely to the Spirit's control.

2. **"The fruit of the Spirit."** When we allow the Holy Spirit to work in us, He produces spiritual fruit that's like a ripe cluster of grapes. This cluster has nine virtues that brighten our lives. The first three, "love, joy, [and] peace" (v. 22a), concern our relationship to God. He is our first love and our first joy, and because of Him we are at peace. The next triad, "patience, kindness, [and] goodness" (v. 22b), describe our relationships with other people. We will seek their best and put up with their worst. And the final three qualities, "faithfulness, gentleness, [and] self-control" (vv. 22b–23a), concern our self-ward relationship. We are able to master our passions and maintain a godly lifestyle. "There is no law" against these virtues (v. 23b); since they are not fleshly, they do not need to be restrained.

> *Facts about Spiritual Fruit*
>
> "Fruit is the result of a long organic and living process. The process is complex and intricate. Fruits are not something made, manufactured or engineered. They are not the product of the drawing board.... They are the results of a life of faith created by God.
> ... We do not produce [fruit] by our own effort. We do not purchase it from another. It is not a reward for doing good deeds, like a merit badge, a gold medal, a blue ribbon. Fruits are simply there. Sometimes we experience them in another, sometimes in ourselves. We live in a world that is mostly result, and so we live in adoration, in awe, in reverence.
> These nine [virtues] are also like fruit in that they are perishable. They spoil. They are beautiful to observe but cannot be kept on display for long. They must be used—eaten and digested. Fruit is something our bodies use to supply the nutrients to live well. Just so, the

2. James Montgomery Boice, "Galatians," in *The Expositor's Bible Commentary,* 12 vols., ed. Frank E. Gaebelein (Grand Rapids, Mich.: Zondervan Publishing House, 1976), vol. 10, p. 497.

Spirit gifts are what we take into our lives so that we are able to live creatively."[3]

C. **The way to victory.** What can we do to overcome this raging war between good and evil? We must side with good and "walk by the Spirit" (vv. 16a, 25b). This process involves two actions that must become as basic to our lives as breathing.

    1. **We must remember that our flesh has been crucified** (v. 24). This means that our sinful nature is dying, not dead. It has been nailed to Christ's cross, so it does not have the power over us it once enjoyed. Yet it can still influence us if we don't let it die. Too often,

> we keep wistfully returning to the scene of its execution. We begin to fondle it, to caress it, to long for its release, even to try to take it down again from the cross. We need to learn to leave it there. When some jealous, or proud, or malicious, or impure thought invades our mind we must kick it out at once. It is fatal to begin to examine it and consider whether we are going to give in to it or not. We have declared war on it; we are not going to resume negotiations.... We have crucified the flesh; we are never going to draw the nails.[4]

    2. **We must walk under the control of the Holy Spirit** (vv. 16, 18, 25). Just as the Holy Spirit led Christ during His temptations in the wilderness (Luke 4:1–2), so the Spirit will guide us through our battle with the flesh. But we must choose to follow His lead and walk along the path of Christian virtue, not retreat into the traps of fleshly indulgence. This process includes focusing our minds on whatever is true, honorable, right, pure, lovely, attractive, excellent, and praiseworthy (Phil. 4:8). For whatever occupies our thoughts permeates who we are (Prov. 23:7a).

III. The Walk Maintained

Perhaps you find yourself swaying on the high wire of Christian liberty. Or maybe you are grasping the platform of legalism or falling into the darkness of licentious living. Regardless of your situation, if you are in Christ, you can regain and maintain your balance by making this counsel an essential part of your daily training.

3. Eugene H. Peterson, *Traveling Light: Reflections on the Free Life* (Downers Grove, Ill.: Inter-Varsity Press, 1982), p. 166.

4. Stott, *The Message of Galatians,* pp. 151–52.

A. Resolve anew each morning to walk in the Spirit. Every day, even before you get up, commit yourself to His control.

B. Strive to maintain your walk throughout each day. Don't turn away from the Spirit's lead so you can flirt with the flesh or with legalism. Walking the tightrope of freedom has its difficulties, but none of them compare to the hazards of going your own way. The Spirit will guide, protect, and empower you. All you must do is follow Him by faith.

 Living Insights

Study One

Have you ever watched little ones taking their first steps? It's quite an adventure! If you watch carefully, you'll notice they have to learn both what and what not to do. Galatians 5:16–25 tells us much about how to walk with God and how not to walk. Let's learn how to improve our pace by observing some of the pitfalls and benefits along the way.

• Make five observations about the flesh.

1. _____

2. _____

3. _____

4. _____

5. _____

• Make five observations about the Spirit.

1. _____

2. _____

3. _____

4. _____

5. _____

• Make five observations about your role in the battle between the flesh and the Spirit.

1. _____

2. _____

3. _____

4. _____

5. _____

🐚 *Living Insights*

Familiar Bible passages can lose their meaning with repetition. We hear them so often that we forget the power they hold. Unfortunately, this portion of Galatians is no exception. Let's look at the fruit of the Spirit as if we've never seen it before.

- Read through the list of virtues in Galatians 5:22–23. Can you think of an example of each of these traits in your life?

_____

_____

_____

- Practically speaking, how do you act upon the fact that your flesh has been crucified?

_____

_____

_____

- Walking under the Spirit's control is the key to victory. Do you know how to walk? Have you learned something in this study that you didn't know before? Do you realize your walk must be started anew each day? Do you maintain it during the day? If so, how?

_____

_____

_____

_____

Gentle Restoration

Galatians 5:26–6:5

Jesus said, " 'Blessed are the gentle, for they shall inherit the earth' " (Matt. 5:5). Is this true? Not if you imbibe today's popular philosophies: Look out for number one . . . win through intimidation . . . capitalize on the blunders of others. Meekness is weakness; severity is strength. The world is a jungle with no room for wimps. If you're going to survive, you must beat out the others, fighting tooth and nail with no regard for the so-called rights and sensitivities of others.

But consider Moses, who in his day was the most humble man on earth (Num. 12:3). With God's power he brought Egypt to its knees and led more than two million Hebrews out of slavery.[1] And yet, when his brother and sister openly challenged his leadership, he didn't defend himself or remind them that they owed their positions to him. Nor did he tell them to shut up or ship out (vv. 1–9). Instead,

> he chose to show great strength and reserve. . . . He held his peace. . . . Moses made no attempt to explain his unique status with God. In fact, we would never have known about it if God Himself had not taken Moses' critics to one side and set the record straight. It takes a certain kind of restraint and strength to refuse to brag, to live humbly with honor, and to choose not to use weapons of defense that would blow the opposition out of the water.[2]

And then there's Jesus, who described Himself as " 'gentle and humble in heart' " (Matt. 11:29). He silenced raging storms, set demons on the run, stood strong against prideful religionists, and exercised power over disease and death. Yet when He was tried on trumped-up charges, threatened with execution, and verbally and physically abused, He refused to lash out with the incredible power at His disposal. He didn't even offer a verbal defense. Instead, He "kept entrusting Himself to Him who judges righteously" (1 Pet. 2:23b). He went to the cross, cried out for God to forgive His executioners, and gave up His life for us (v. 24, Luke 23:33–48).

Gentleness gets a bum rap today. But the lives of Moses and Jesus demonstrate that strength under control accomplishes more good than selfishness out of control. The Apostle Paul agrees. Let's examine what he says about this Christian virtue in his letter to the Galatian church.

---

1. See John J. Davis's *Moses and the Gods of Egypt: Studies in the Book of Exodus* (Grand Rapids, Mich.: Baker Book House, 1971), p. 146.
2. D. Stuart Briscoe, *Spirit Life* (Old Tappan, N.J.: Fleming H. Revell Co., 1983), pp. 124–25.

I. True Spirituality

"The fruit of the Spirit," says Paul, "is love, joy, peace, patience, kindness, goodness, faithfulness, *gentleness*, self-control; against such things there is no law" (Gal. 5:22–23, emphasis added). When we walk in the Spirit, gentleness will characterize our lives. We will find our pride subdued, our submission to God heightened, and our concern for others deepened. Self-assertion will take a backseat to self-control. Fists will open, index fingers will stop jabbing others in the chest, and sneers will give way to words of comfort and encouragement. Are these signs of character weakness or flabbiness? No way! It is much easier to give in to the flesh and produce "enmities, strife, jealousy, outbursts of anger, disputes, dissensions, factions, [and] envying" (vv. 20–21a). Anyone can be fleshly, but only Christians can be truly spiritual.

II. Spirit-filled Involvement

The Galatian Christians were guilty of infighting due to divisions apparently caused by the Judaizers. So Paul urges them to put their dissensions aside and start living spiritually. His counsel to them also has tremendous bearing on how we should treat one another.

A. How *not* to treat one another. "Let us not become boastful, challenging one another, envying one another" (v. 26). Conceit folds its arms across its chest and boasts, "I'm better than you and I'll prove it." Inferiority sticks its hands in its pockets and mumbles, "You're better than I am and I resent it." Paul challenges both attitudes. Neither superiority nor jealousy has any place in the Christian life. Both are results of the flesh, not products of the Spirit.

B. How *to* treat one another. So how should we behave in the Body of Christ? The answer is tied up with how we see ourselves.

1. **We should help each other carry burdensome loads.** We are to "bear one another's burdens, and thus fulfill the law of Christ" (6:2). None of us are totally self-reliant. At times, life depresses us and temptation threatens to crush us. Our knees begin to buckle under the oppressive weight of our loads. During these struggles we need other believers to come alongside to help share our burden. Conversely, when we see fellow Christians wavering under the strain of their loads, we need to come to their aid and help shoulder the weight. As we both give and receive this kind of ministry, we will "fulfill the law of Christ," which is to love others as He loved us (John 13:34) and as we love ourselves (Gal. 5:14).

2. **We should appraise ourselves accurately.** Pride and inferiority can block the ministry of burden-bearing. Both can lead us to hide our struggles, leaving us to suffer under them

on our own or to unload them onto God's shoulders only. Certainly, the Lord is strong enough and wants to bear our burdens. But when they become unbearable for us, He wants us to go beyond sharing them with Him or keeping them to ourselves. He wants us to give other Christians an opportunity to shoulder some of our load. In fact, this is a major avenue God uses to rush needed relief to us. So in order to remove the roadblocks of pride and inferiority, we need to have an accurate self-concept. We need to avoid both inflated and deflated perceptions of ourselves, both of which lead to self-deception (6:3). We should step back and take an objective look at ourselves and our accomplishments. Then when we find character traits and deeds that are Spirit-produced, we can rejoice in them without feeling superior or inferior to others. The only standard we should ever compare ourselves to is Christ, who is manifested through the Spirit's fruit. All other standards are mere shadows or perversions.[3]

3. **We should shoulder what we can.** Another barrier to the burden-bearing ministry is freeloading. We can shirk our God-given responsibilities, piling them on fellow Christians. Instead of carrying what we can, we weigh down others with a double load. God will not let us get away with this. As Paul states, "Each one shall bear his own load" (v. 5). John Stott makes some helpful observations regarding this verse:

> There is no contradiction here between verse 2, 'Bear one another's burdens', and verse 5, 'each man will have to bear his own load'. The Greek word for burden is different, *baros* (verse 2) meaning a weight or heavy load and *phortion* (verse 5) being 'a common term for a man's pack'. So we are to bear one another's 'burdens' which are too heavy for a man to bear alone, but there is one burden which we cannot share—indeed do not need to because it is a pack light enough for every man to carry himself—and that is our responsibility to God on the day of judgment. On that day you cannot carry my pack and I cannot carry yours. 'Each man will have to bear his own load.'[4]

3. An excellent treatment of self-assessment is given by Josh McDowell in his book *His Image My Image* (San Bernardino, Calif.: Here's Life Publishers, 1984).

4. John R. W. Stott, *The Message of Galatians: Only One Way,* The Bible Speaks Today series (Downers Grove, Ill.: InterVarsity Press, 1968), pp. 159–60.

We are each accountable to God for how we live. Try as we might, we cannot pass off our obligations to others. We need to carry our share of the load and seek or accept help only when we really need it.

III. Gentle Confrontation

To help us better understand this burden-bearing ministry, Paul addresses the Christian who has discovered a fallen believer—a person who has been overtaken and caught by sin.[5] The main thrust of Paul's counsel is that fallen kindred should be gently picked up, brushed off, and encouraged to renew their pilgrimage. With this in mind, let's consider the details of his advice.

A. Who should do it? "Brethren, even if a man is caught in any trespass, you who are spiritual, restore such a one in a spirit of gentleness" (v. 1a). Notice that Paul doesn't say only deacons, elders, pastors, or professional counselors can handle these cases. There are no vocational, sexual, racial, or social criteria for helping a wayward believer get back on the right road. The only requirement is spirituality. The restorer must be a Christian who displays the fruit of the Spirit (5:22–23).

B. How should it be done? Put simply, with gentleness and humility (6:1). Fallen Christians are not to be slapped around, humiliated, reviled, or ignored. That's the approach of the flesh; that's what pride or inferiority would lead us to do. Rather, these fellow believers need to be handled with the attitude that says, But for the grace of God, there go I. None of us are immune to sin. The disease infects us all; at times, it gains the upper hand. When a believer is suffering, we should follow Martin Luther's advice: " 'Run unto him, and reaching out your hand, raise him up again, comfort him with sweet words, and embrace him with motherly arms.' "[6] We should talk straight but bathe our words in love.

C. What is the goal? Restoration (v. 1a). The word Paul uses is the verb *katartizō*. It was used for setting a fractured bone or mending a torn fishing net. The word's stress is on repair or cure; its central idea is replacing what is needed in order to bring effectiveness again. What do fallen Christians need? Loving confrontation, understanding, encouragement, and companionship. They need someone who will stick by them and help share their burden until the weight is reduced to a bearable level.

5. See Donald K. Campbell's commentary "Galatians" in *The Bible Knowledge Commentary: New Testament,* ed. John F. Walvoord and Roy B. Zuck (Wheaton, Ill.: Victor Books, 1983), p. 609.

6. Martin Luther, *Commentary on the Epistle to the Galatians,* as quoted by Stott in *The Message of Galatians,* pp. 160–61.

D. Why is the process so delicate? Three answers come to mind. First, the process involves human beings. We are fragile, complicated creatures who, unlike animals, bear God's image (Gen. 1:27) and therefore deserve to be treated with great dignity (Ps. 8:3–8). Second, we are not perfect models of righteousness. We all fight with the flesh, experience temporary defeats, and need to be helped up, not held down, when we're nursing our wounds. And third, delicacy is required because the purpose of the process is to mend, not cripple. It's painful enough to be trapped by sin. We don't need fellow Christians to enter our lives and inflict more pain than we're already suffering.

Healing the Wounded

Do you know another Christian caught in the jaws of sin? Don't run from the scene or stand on the sidelines feeling smug. Realize that one day you may be in the same situation—bleeding from a temptation that got the better of you. First examine yourself to see if you're a qualified physician. Does your bedside manner exhibit "love, joy, peace, patience, kindness, goodness, faithfulness, gentleness, [and] self-control" (Gal. 5:22–23a)? You may not have these traits in abundance, but they should be present. Are they? If so, go to that person's aid and, using the instruments of gentleness and humility, treat the injury and nurse your patient back to health. But if your self-examination shows that you are not qualified to administer aid, tactfully seek out someone who is. In this way you can still play a significant role in healing the wounded.

 Living Insights

Study One

Galatians 6:1 makes an unmistakable link between spirituality and gentleness. As we are controlled by the Spirit, we *will* exhibit the virtue of gentleness. Let's pursue a greater understanding of this biblical quality.

• The New Testament verses listed here all address gentleness. Look up each one and jot down your observations.

Gentleness

Matthew 5:5 _____

_____

2 Corinthians 10:1 _____

_____

Galatians 5:23 _____

_____

Colossians 3:12 _____

_____

1 Timothy 3:2–3 _____

_____

2 Timothy 2:24–25 _____

_____

James 3:13 _____

_____

1 Peter 3:3–4 _____

_____

1 Peter 3:15 _____

_____

- Based on your observations, how would you define the biblical concept of gentleness?

_____

_____

_____

Continued on next page

121

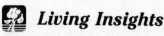 *Living Insights*

Confrontation should be done by spiritual people in gentleness and humility in order to restore. We must deal delicately with fellow Christians, for we're all imperfect.

- Has God brought to mind someone who needs loving confrontation? Have you examined your heart, making sure you possess the necessary spiritual qualities? If so, watch out for the extremes. Don't run from confrontation; but on the other hand, don't be overly anxious. You may want to collect your thoughts by asking yourself, How can I confront this person in love? Remember Proverbs 15:28: "The heart of the righteous ponders how to answer, / But the mouth of the wicked pours out evil things."

The Law of the Harvest
Galatians 6:6–10

What would you think if someone told you, "If your diet consists mainly of foods high in cholesterol and fat, you will lose weight"? What about, "Drinking a quart of alcohol a day will keep you from becoming an alcoholic"? Or "By refusing to meet new people, you're bound to make new friends"? You would probably think the person making these statements was crazy, confused, ignorant, or joking. And you'd be right. People who eat a lot of foods high in fat and cholesterol gain weight. Heavy drinkers become alcoholics. Social hermits become friendless. Similarly, people who eat and drink in moderation and attempt to make friends don't become obese, alcoholic, or reclusive. Why? Because we reap what we sow. If we want to achieve certain goals, we must do what it takes to reach them. And if we wish to avoid certain consequences, we must refuse to do anything that would lead to those results.

With rare exceptions, this principle holds true in everything we do.[1] Yet as often as we observe this law in action, we are frequently surprised or even angered when it crops up in our Christian walk. We think we can sin and then escape the consequences through prayer or renewed commitment to God. Sometimes the Lord will grant our request; however, most of the time, He won't. And for good reason. We will never learn to hate sin and love serving God if we rarely experience sin's consequences.

In his epistle to the Galatian Christians, Paul brings this principle to the forefront and urges us to order our lives with it in mind. He reminds us that this law is a two-edged sword: it can bring reward or punishment, holiness or corruption. Everything depends on what we choose to sow.

I. Harvest Laws

The principle that states you reap what you sow is best illustrated in farming. In fact, four agricultural laws revolve around the almost universal validity of this one principle.

A. We reap what we plant. Since the beginning of life on earth, like has begotten like (Gen. 1:11–12, 21–22, 24–28). Dogs have given birth to dogs, birds to birds, fish to fish, and humans to

---

1. The biblical principle of reaping what one sows should not be confused with the Eastern concept of the law of karma. Karma is viewed as an unbreakable, universal law of cause and effect that says for every action there is a corresponding reaction. The deeds we perform in this life will inexorably determine the condition of our lives hereafter. The biblical law is not as deterministic as the karmic one. According to Scripture, our present deeds do impact our future but, unlike karmic law, there is room for God's forgiveness and deliverance. A complete discussion of this issue is provided by Norman L. Geisler and J. Yutaka Amano in their book *The Reincarnation Sensation* (Wheaton, Ill.: Tyndale House Publishers, 1986).

humans.[2] The same holds true in farming. From watermelon seeds come watermelons, from orange trees, oranges, and from grapevines, grapes. If you want grapes, you don't plant orange trees. And if you want watermelons, you don't try to get them from grapevines. That's the way God created His world to operate, and He won't change it simply because we might want Him to.

B. We reap in a different season than when we plant. We can't harvest a crop before or at the same time it's planted. Harvesting always follows a season of planting and growth. Solomon puts it poetically: "There is . . . A time to plant, and a time to uproot what is planted" (Eccles. 3:1–2). Try as we might, we can't bypass this process.

C. We reap more than we plant. A peach tree produces many peaches; a grapevine bears bunches of grapes; one stalk of corn yields several ears. This inherent ability in plants goes all the way back to their divine creation (Gen. 1:11–12).

D. We can do nothing about last year's harvest, but we can do something about next year's. We can't change the past. Once a harvest is in, its quality and quantity are set. We can, however, take steps that will improve the production of our next crop. Although some factors will always be outside our control, we are responsible to handle wisely what is under our influence.

Living by Harvest Laws

These four laws are just as applicable to the Christian life as they are to agriculture. Consider the first two laws. Centuries ago one of Job's friends observed, "Those who plow iniquity / And those who sow trouble harvest it" (Job 4:8). The fruit of our actions won't always come quickly. But all things remaining equal, the produce will come eventually, and it will be what we planted.

The third law—we reap more than we plant—was graphically stated by Hosea: "They sow the wind, / And they reap the whirlwind" (Hos. 8:7a). When we shrug off God's counsel and go our own way, in due time the consequences of our choice will swirl around us, threatening to blow us down.

Then there's the fourth law. Even though yesterday's actions are irreversible, tomorrow's are not. We can dramatically affect our future by the decisions we make today.

---

2. Scientific confirmation of this truth is given in *Fossils in Focus,* by J. Kerby Anderson and Harold G. Coffin (Grand Rapids, Mich.: Zondervan Publishing House, 1977; Richardson, Tex.: Probe Ministries International, 1977); and *The Natural Limits to Biological Change,* by Lane P. Lester and Raymond G. Bohlin (Grand Rapids, Mich.: Zondervan Publishing House, 1984).

II. The Christian Life

In Galatians 6:6–10, Paul draws on the harvest law that states you reap what you sow to address the financial and social responsibility of Christians.

A. A command regarding giving. Paul opens this section with an exhortation directed at the recipients of a teaching ministry: "Let the one who is taught the word share all good things with him who teaches" (v. 6). The person who sows the seed of God's Word should expect to reap a livelihood. It makes no difference whether the instructor is a missionary, minister, evangelist, private tutor, or schoolteacher. Students should help supply their teachers' material needs. As Paul says in 1 Corinthians: "If we have sown spiritual seed among you, is it too much if we reap a material harvest from you?... The Lord has commanded that those who preach the gospel should receive their living from the gospel" (9:11–14).[3] This command can be abused by both teachers and students. Take a church, for example. Her pastor can become lazy or ineffective and still receive his salary. On the other hand, his congregation can use his salary to coerce him into preaching what they want to hear. Both situations are wrong, and both can be avoided if ministers and their congregations diligently pursue their responsibilities according to biblical guidelines.[4] It will also help if teachers and students develop a proper perspective of each other. In Galatians 6:6, the Greek word translated "share" is *koinōnía,* which means "fellowship" or "partnership." Teachers and students are partners in the same investment—presenting and applying God's Word. So they need to do their different parts to ensure the continuation of the ministry. When both parties do what they should, both will share in the teaching ministry's abundant fruit.

B. A reminder of the harvest law. Paul now turns from the subject of giving to personal holiness, with the harvest law still on his mind. "Do not be deceived, God is not mocked; for whatever a man sows, this he will also reap" (v. 7). We can't fool or ridicule God. Though we may plant one kind of lifestyle and hope to harvest the produce of another, we will be disappointed. God will not overturn His law. "The one who sows to his own flesh shall from the flesh reap corruption, but the one who sows to

---

3. *The NIV Study Bible* (Grand Rapids, Mich.: Zondervan Bible Publishers, 1985).

4. This point is developed in these sources: *Excellence in Ministry,* ed. Bill Watkins, from the Bible-teaching ministry of Charles R. Swindoll (Fullerton, Calif.: Insight for Living, 1985); *Sharpening the Focus of the Church,* by Gene A. Getz (Chicago, Ill.: Moody Press, 1974); and *A New Testament Blueprint for the Church,* by John Moore and Ken Neff (Chicago, Ill.: Moody Press, 1985).

the Spirit shall from the Spirit reap eternal life" (v. 8). We cannot expect to harvest the field of holiness if we plant in the field of carnality. Even divine forgiveness may not thwart the consequences of this law. David's sin with Bathsheba is a case in point. The Israelite king requested and received God's pardon for committing adultery and murder. Yet the consequences of his sin wreaked havoc in both his private and public life. God didn't stop or even slow down the results; indeed, He initiated some of them as part of David's punishment (2 Sam. 11–23).

C. Encouragement to continue. Paul now moves from the personal to the communal: "Let us not lose heart in doing good, for in due time we shall reap if we do not grow weary. So then, while we have opportunity, let us do good to all men, and especially to those who are of the household of the faith" (Gal. 6:9–10). Sleepless nights and frustrating days can accompany caring for a crop and meeting people's needs. Both endeavors can seem endless and thankless. But just as a crop will eventually produce a harvest, so acts of kindness will one day lead to a rich reward—one that is beyond our wildest imaginations (Matt. 5:12, 25:14–23, 31–34; 2 Tim. 4:7–8; 1 Pet. 5:4). In his exhortation Paul encourages us to do good to all people, especially those who are Christians (Gal. 6:10).

> Is that selfish? Shortsighted? No. Paul doesn't direct our attention to those who are close to home because they are more deserving but because they are *there,* and he knows that the biggest deterrent to the drudgery of caring for an everyday friend is the dreaming of helping an exotic stranger. Giving from a distance requires less of us—less involvement, less compassion. It is easier to write out a check for a starving child halfway around the world than to share the burden of our next-door neighbor who talks too much. The distant child makes a slight dent in my checkbook; the neighbor interferes with my routines and my sleep. . . .
>
> Paul will not permit us to compensate for neglecting those nearest us by advertising our compassion for those on another continent. Jesus, it must be remembered, restricted nine-tenths of his ministry to twelve Jews because it was the only way to redeem all Americans. He couldn't be bothered . . . with the foreign Canaanites because his work was to save the whole world. The check for the starving child must still be written and the missionary sent, but as an

extension of what we are doing at home, not as an *exemption* from it.[5]

III. Our Lives Today

These four verses in Galatians are packed with seed for thought. But let's remove them from the realm of the mind and plant them in the soil of action.

A. Let's share our finances. We need to relax our grip on our funds and invest them in the lives of those who feed our souls. And we should give to our teachers proportionately, not only in relation to their needs, but also with regard to the measure in which they meet *our* needs. Those who help us most in our walk with God should receive the largest share of our giving.

B. Let's sow in the Spirit, not in the flesh. Holiness begets holiness; wickedness begets wickedness. We must stop sowing wild oats during the week and praying for a crop failure on Sunday. If we really want to enjoy the fruit of the Spirit, we need to plant our lives in His field.

C. Let's not grow tired of doing good. If we weary of sowing good works, we will end up like farmers who quit planting because they're impatient. We will reap only a small portion of the harvest we could have had. We need to encourage ourselves and each other to keep on keeping on in the spiritual sowing process (compare Heb. 10:24–25).

D. Let's do good to all, especially to those closest to us. Some people are easy to serve; others are more difficult. No one knows that better than Jesus Christ. He came to sow seeds of faith in the field of sinful humanity. Although some people readily accepted Him, most rejected Him, and many crucified Him. But in time, the seeds He had planted took root and began to sprout. The Church was born, and for centuries she has harvested the souls Christ cultivated. The Lord has called us to work with Him in the field of humanity. Sometimes we will toil and yet not see the fruit of our labor in this life; at other times, we will reap the benefits of another's toil. But Jesus told us this will happen so that " 'he who sows and he who reaps may rejoice together' " (John 4:36b). Let's reach out to everyone we can, giving all we are and have to the service of our Lord—the farmer who cannot fail.

5. Eugene H. Peterson, *Traveling Light: Reflections on the Free Life* (Downers Grove, Ill.: InterVarsity Press, 1982), pp. 181–82.

Living Insights

The simplicity and depth of the Bible are stunning ironies. Some principles are clearly visible, but so much buried treasure still waits to be brought to the surface. This section of Galatians presents practical truths. Let's grab a shovel and see if we can uncover more hidden treasure.

• Listed below are some key words and phrases from Galatians 6:6–10. Look up some cross-references on the same subject and jot down your observations.

Galatians 6:6–10

"One who is taught the word" Cross-references: _____

Observations: _____

_____

_____

"Share" Cross-references: _____

Observations: _____

_____

_____

"God is not mocked" Cross-references: _____

Observations: _____

_____

_____

"Reap corruption" Cross-references: _____

Observations: _____

_____

_____

"Sows to the Spirit" Cross-references: _____

Observations: _____

_____

_____

"Reap eternal life"   Cross-references: _____

Observations: _____

_____

_____

"Not lose heart in doing good" Cross-references: _____

Observations: _____

_____

_____

"Opportunity"   Cross-references: _____

Observations: _____

_____

_____

"Do good to all men"   Cross-references: _____

Observations: _____

_____

_____

"Household of the faith"   Cross-references: _____

Observations: _____

_____

_____

Continued on next page

Living Insights

Four principles are communicated in Galatians 6:6–10. Just as the believers of Galatia needed to be reminded of them, so do we.

- Check (✓) the answers that best describe your life today.

My Life Today			
Applications	Doing Great	Needs Work	Don't Ask
Share Finances	☐	☐	☐
Sow in the Spirit, Not in the Flesh	☐	☐	☐
Don't Grow Tired of Doing Good	☐	☐	☐
Do Good to All	☐	☐	☐

- Are you doing all right in these areas? Do some of them need work? Does "don't ask" summarize your situation? Perhaps some of these qualities are missing from your life. Why do you think this has happened?

  _____

  _____

  _____

- To help develop these principles more consistently in your life, complete the following statements:

  The principle I'll begin working on is: _____

  _____

  Three ways I can apply this command are:

  1. _____

  2. _____

  3. _____

  The person who could best help me meet my objectives is:

  _____

A Bold, Blunt Reproof
Galatians 6:11–16

When we want to emphasize something we've written, we can use exclamation points, dashes, underlines, or capital letters. The New Testament writers did not use any of these methods. In the first century, Greek was written in uncials—boxlike letters similar to English capitals—and the words were generally run together without punctuation or spaces. So when a New Testament writer wished to highlight certain words, he would frequently place them at the beginning of the sentence. Or sometimes he would simply pen the words in a bolder style.[1] Paul used this latter approach in the closing verses of his letter to the Galatian Christians.

Throughout this letter, Paul has dictated his thoughts to an unknown amanuensis. But beginning in chapter 6, verse 11, he takes the pen from his secretary's hand and bears down on the parchment, conveying his final thoughts with dark, bold strokes. Undoubtedly, his handwriting would verify to the Galatian Christians that this letter was indeed from Paul. More than this, however, the "large letters" would stand out from the rest of the letter, causing these believers to pay particular attention to Paul's final remarks.

As we examine what Paul has emphasized, we will see that it involves not only a brief review of his letter but also a blunt reproof directed toward the Judaizers—those who had embraced legalism rather than the Christian gospel.

I. Facing the Facts

One last time, Paul spells out the difference between salvation by works and salvation by faith. He contrasts outward and inward religion, human and divine work, and self-centered and Christ-centered living.

A. Outward or inward religion. The Judaizers had entered the Galatian congregation and convinced many of its members to live according to the Mosaic Law. These legalists told them that in order to be saved they had to undergo circumcision and obey the remainder of the Law. Legalists today still add conditions to faith in Christ—conditions like water baptism, church membership, or obedience to "new revelations." Concerning the

---

1. More information on the writing and development of the New Testament can be found in these sources: *History of the New Testament in Plain Language,* by Clayton Harrop (Waco, Tex.: Word Books, 1984); *A General Introduction to the Bible,* rev. ed., by Norman L. Geisler and William E. Nix (Chicago, Ill.: Moody Press, 1986); and *Scribes, Scrolls, and Scripture: A Student's Guide to New Testament Textual Criticism,* by J. Harold Greenlee (Grand Rapids, Mich.: William B. Eerdmans Publishing Co., 1985).

Judaizers, Paul says: "Those who want to make a good impression outwardly are trying to compel you to be circumcised. The only reason they do this is to avoid being persecuted for the cross of Christ. Not even those who are circumcised obey the law, yet they want you to be circumcised that they may boast about your flesh" (Gal. 6:12–13).[2] Like contemporary legalists, the Judaizers were concerned only with externals—how things appeared on the surface, not how they were deep within. They were like the Pharisees who prayed and donated loudly and publicly so they would be applauded by others (Matt. 6:1–5). All that mattered to them was human approval and praise. Why was this so important to them? Paul gives two reasons.

1. **The Judaizers wanted to avoid persecution** (Gal. 6:12b). Christ's crucifixion was "a stumbling block" to the Jews (1 Cor. 1:23). They were looking for a political messiah who would forcefully deliver them from the Roman government.[3] Instead, a man came preaching love and peace, upsetting the established Jewish religious order. Then He died as a criminal on a cross at the hands of the Romans. To add insult to injury, Jesus and His followers claimed that His death was necessary for man's salvation. No one could be made right with God unless they claimed Christ's death as payment for sin. Unbelieving Jews found this teaching extremely offensive, and they did everything they could to wipe Christianity off the face of the earth. As Paul did before his conversion, many Jews sought out believers to imprison or kill. The Judaizers tried to escape this onslaught by mixing a pharisaic form of Judaism with Christianity. But Paul understands that any compromise with authentic Christianity is far more disastrous than suffering ridicule, imprisonment, or even execution. One's eternal destiny is at stake.

2. **The Judaizers were obsessed with ecclesiastical statistics** (Gal. 6:13b).

> The legalizers wanted to boast in the flesh of the Galatians. This means that they wanted to boast in the number of circumcisions, much as David had boasted in the two hundred foreskins of the Philistines. They were trophy hunters and wanted to be able to report on mass "conversions" in Galatia. The humbling parallel would be in the

2. *The NIV Study Bible* (Grand Rapids, Mich.: Zondervan Bible Publishers, 1985).

3. See *The Life of Christ,* by Robert Duncan Culver (Grand Rapids, Mich.: Baker Book House, 1976); and *Jesus and the Zealots,* by S. G. F. Brandon (New York, N.Y.: Charles Scribner's Sons, 1967).

tendency to take pride in counting the number
of "decisions for Christ" or "baptisms" today.[4]

B. Human or divine work. In contrast to the Judaizers, Paul
sees only one thing worth boasting about: "the cross of our Lord
Jesus Christ" (v. 14a). The shadow it had cast over his life led
him into the noonday light of salvation by faith alone. Now
everything he had once valued highly was like reeking garbage
when compared to the cross (Phil. 3:7–8). Neither circumcision,
water baptism, church membership, obedience to the Law, nor
adhering to a new list of dos and don'ts makes any difference
as far as our relationship to God is concerned. The only thing
that matters is whether or not we have become new creations
through Christ's death (Gal. 6:15). People who love getting strokes
for their own efforts find this message offensive, but if they don't
accept it by faith alone, they are doomed to spend eternity in
the darkness of their own selfishness. C. S. Lewis says it well:

> The characteristic of lost souls is "their rejection of
> everything that is not simply themselves." Our imag-
> inary egoist has tried to turn everything he meets
> into a province or appendage of the self. The taste
> for the *other*, that is, the very capacity for enjoying
> good, is quenched in him except in so far as his body
> still draws him into some rudimentary contact with
> an outer world. Death removes this last contact. He
> has his wish—to live wholly in the self and to make
> the best of what he finds there. And what he finds
> there is Hell.[5]

C. Self-centered or Christ-centered living. Paul states that
"those who will walk by this rule"—the measuring stick of Christ's
cross—will have "peace and mercy" (v. 16). Only a life reborn
and growing in Jesus can experience peace and mercy instead
of turmoil and judgment. People who live for themselves or any
other human standard are at enmity with God and living under
His decree of judgment. And although on the surface they may
appear to have their lives all put together, underneath they are
living lives of quiet desperation.

II. Responding to the Truth

Paul's message in the closing section of his letter leaves us with two
thoughts we need to consider.

---

4. James Montgomery Boice, "Galatians," in *The Expositor's Bible Commentary,* 12 vols., ed.
Frank E. Gaebelein (Grand Rapids, Mich.: Zondervan Publishing House, 1976), vol. 10, pp. 506–7.

5. C. S. Lewis, *The Problem of Pain* (New York, N.Y.: Macmillan Publishing Co., 1962), p. 123.

A. In our do-it-yourself society, salvation by grace is easily rejected. Our culture teaches that we must earn our own way . . . that hard work will get us where we want to go . . . that anything worthwhile is achieved with a lot of sweat. Then we are told by some people that the greatest prize in life can be ours by simply believing in the sacrifice of another. This message assaults our humanistic mind-set. We jeer at those who dare to suggest this ridiculous idea. But as Paul has made so plain, the only thing we gain by working for our own salvation is ourselves, separated eternally from God.

B. In God's plan, the only way we are saved is through Christ's finished work on the cross. Jesus has achieved what we cannot. He has completely paid our debt to God; He has provided for our release from the curse and demands of the Law; He has made it possible for us to become free to serve the Lord. All we must do to receive these incredible benefits is accept Christ by faith. Believe in Him—that's all there is to it. Have you put your trust in Him yet? If not, what are you waiting for? Heaven rather than hell can be your destiny if you'll simply place your life in Christ's hands. Don't put it off any longer.

Living Insights

Study One

"But may it never be that I should boast, except in the cross of our Lord Jesus Christ" (Gal. 6:14a). Pride in human achievement has plagued man since the Fall. Rather than emphasize God's work in our lives, we frequently boast and glory in our own achievements.

* Many a Bible character has also wrestled with pride. Read through the following accounts and summarize how haughtiness has reared its ugly head.

Adam and Eve—Genesis 3

Summary: _____

_____

_____

_____

Samson—Judges 16

Summary: _____

_____

_____

_____

Israelites—1 Samuel 8

Summary: _____

_____

_____

Solomon—1 Kings 11:1–13

Summary: _____

_____

_____

_____

Jonah—Jonah 1, 3–4

Summary: _____

_____

_____

_____

Pharisees—Matthew 23

Summary: _____

_____

_____

_____

Continued on next page

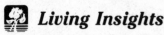 *Living Insights*

This study provides us with one more opportunity to reflect on the beauty of our salvation. It is often rejected on the grounds that it's too simple. But the truth remains: we're acceptable to God only through Christ's work on the cross. Two decisions concerning salvation are discussed below. Take time to deal with the one that is appropriate to your relationship with God.

● Are you ready to accept Christ as your personal Savior? A casual glance at Galatians will quickly demonstrate that human achievement is not required for salvation. Please let this book introduce you to the new life available only in Christ. Here is a brief, easily understood explanation of how you can come to God.

> **Coming to Terms with Christ**
>
> The decision to come to Christ in faith is the most important commitment you will ever make. This decision carries not only eternal hope but significance for day-to-day living as well. That is not a glib statement—it is *reality*.
>
> God knows that we search, struggle, and hurt. He offers us hope, forgiveness, and love. In John 3:16 Jesus states, "For God so loved the world, that He gave His only begotten Son, that whoever believes in Him should not perish, but have eternal life." Christ has paid for your sin by His death on the cross. If you are uncertain about your relationship with God, pause and tell Him that you acknowledge His Son as your Savior. Accepting Christ is neither complicated nor mysterious.
>
> The Bible promises that you become God's child *forever* as a result of your trust in Christ. You are significant to God. Begin your walk with Him today.
>
> If you have made this decision and have no one near you with whom you can share, write and let us know. We want to encourage you!

● If you are a believer, do you know someone who needs to learn the liberating message of Galatians? Why not use this time to think of an effective way to reach this person for Christ? Yes, *you* be the one to share! Much of what you've learned in these lessons can equip you to communicate the key issue—salvation is through grace, not works. Go in God's strength and wisdom.

A Branded Man

Galatians 6:17–18, 2 Corinthians 11:23–28

From beginning to end, the Bible claims God as its author. "All Scripture is God-breathed" (2 Tim. 3:16a),[1] so, regardless of where our eyes fall on its pages, we see the very words, the very thoughts of the Lord Himself.

Yet it is also true that the Bible is a human book. Men such as Moses, Joshua, David, Solomon, Luke, and Paul expressed their thoughts and feelings in writing. Certainly, God oversaw what they penned and kept them from making errors of any kind. But with rare exceptions, He did not treat the biblical writers as mere secretaries, dictating to them what He wanted said. Instead, He used their individual characteristics to communicate His Word to man. And as theologian Gordon Lewis points out, the human authors had many differences.

> Each was conditioned by factors distinctive of his time and place. Each had a distinctive heredity and environment. Each had a distinctive type and level of education or training. Although they all lived basically within a Judeo-Christian cultural environment over some fifteen centuries, they had quite different experiences within that basic culture and with other surrounding cultures. Each had distinctive interests and emphases—evident, for example, in the distinctive approaches of the four Gospels to Christ's life, death, and resurrection. Each had a distinctive vocabulary and writing style. Each reflects a distinctive cluster of natural and spiritual gifts.[2]

Thus, the Bible stands as a uniquely coauthored book. It is truly the Word of God and truly the word of man. It conveys man's humanity as much as it does God's deity.

Paul's humanity flows from the pages of his letter to the Galatian church. As we close our study of this epistle, we will review some of his more intense thoughts and emotions. Then we will complete our study by focusing on the most human part of Galatians—the final two verses.

I. Humanity in Scripture

Before turning to Galatians, let's look at three passages that clearly illustrate the Bible's depth of humanness.

A. Ecclesiastes 2:17–20, 3:18–20. Unlike Solomon's other works—Proverbs and the Song of Solomon—Ecclesiastes is painted in the dark, drab colors of emptiness, frustration, and

---

1. *The NIV Study Bible* (Grand Rapids, Mich.: Zondervan Bible Publishers, 1985).

2. Gordon R. Lewis, "The Human Authorship of Inspired Scripture," in *Inerrancy,* ed. Norman L. Geisler (Grand Rapids, Mich.: Zondervan Publishing House, 1979), p. 249.

despair. The sage describes the utter futility of life lived apart from God. Solomon knows what he's talking about; he tried it. Ecclesiastes is the reflective record of his vigorous attempt.[3] We can catch a glimpse of his struggle in chapter 2:

> I hated life, for the work which had been done under the sun was grievous to me; because everything is futility and striving after wind. Thus I hated all the fruit of my labor for which I had labored under the sun.... Therefore I completely despaired of all the fruit of my labor. (vv. 17–20a)

These are the words of a depressed, disillusioned man. And though his spirits brighten at times, they are usually colored in darker shades. For instance:

> I said to myself concerning the sons of men, "God has surely tested them in order for them to see that they are but beasts." For the fate of the sons of men and the fate of beasts is the same. As one dies so dies the other; indeed, they all have the same breath and there is no advantage for man over beast, for all is vanity. All go to the same place. All came from the dust and all return to the dust. (3:18–20)

Depression and futility are not solely modern-day feelings; even saints of old wrestled with them.

B. Romans 7:15–24. Flipping the pages forward to the New Testament letter of Romans, we discover one of the Bible's most moving descriptions of conflict in the Christian life. Paul bares his soul when he writes:

> I do not understand what I do. For what I want to do I do not do, but what I hate I do. And if I do what I do not want to do, I agree that the law is good. As it is, it is no longer I myself who do it, but it is sin living in me. I know that nothing good lives in me, that is, in my sinful nature. For I have the desire to do what is good, but I cannot carry it out. For what I do is not the good I want to do; no, the evil I do not want to do—this I keep on doing. Now if I do what I do not want to do, it is no longer I who do it, but it is sin living in me that does it.
>   ... What a wretched man I am![4]

Can't we all identify with Paul's experience?

---

3. A practical exposition of Ecclesiastes is given in the study guide *Living on the Ragged Edge: Coming to Terms with Reality,* ed. Bill Watkins, from the Bible-teaching ministry of Charles R. Swindoll (Fullerton, Calif.: Insight for Living, 1986).

4. *The NIV Study Bible.*

C. Second Corinthians 11:23–28. In this passage Paul takes us down the road he has traveled and points to the many perils he has endured for the sake of the gospel.

> Are they servants of Christ? (I speak as if insane) I more so; in far more labors, in far more imprisonments, beaten times without number, often in danger of death. Five times I received from the Jews thirty-nine lashes. Three times I was beaten with rods, once I was stoned, three times I was shipwrecked, a night and a day I have spent in the deep. I have been on frequent journeys, in dangers from rivers, dangers from robbers, dangers from my countrymen, dangers from the Gentiles, dangers in the city, dangers in the wilderness, dangers on the sea, dangers among false brethren; I have been in labor and hardship, through many sleepless nights, in hunger and thirst, often without food, in cold and exposure. Apart from such external things, there is the daily pressure upon me of concern [or worry] for all the churches.

Though most of us will never experience the physical hardship Paul did, we can certainly empathize with the psychological stress he must have endured through his trials.

II. Legalism in Galatia

Returning to Galatians, we can see, even in our brief review, the intense emotion Paul felt while confronting legalism in the Galatian church.

A. "I am amazed" (1:6a). Paul didn't open his letter to the Galatian Christians in his usual style. He skipped all commendations and began by expressing shock—shock over the Galatians' acceptance of the heretical gospel of salvation by works. Then, with stern, uncompromising words, Paul gritted his teeth and told these believers, "Even though we, or an angel from heaven, should preach to you a gospel contrary to that which we have preached to you, let him be [damned]" (v. 8).

B. "You foolish Galatians, who has bewitched you?" (3:1a). Paul knew he had taught these Christians well. So he understood that they were not ignoring the truth but had been conned into accepting error. They had failed to use their powers of perception; consequently, they had been tricked by a theological sleight of hand. Now they were living a contradiction—trying to hold on to grace while pursuing a religion of works. Paul called them idiots for making this attempt.

C. **"How is it that you turn back again?"** (4:9b). Once again, Paul expressed his amazement at the Galatians' decision to adopt a teaching that was antithetical to the Christian gospel. How could they give up their freedom in Christ for bondage to the Law? The idea was ludicrous, and yet they had made that choice. No wonder Paul questioned the value of his ministry to them (v. 11).

D. **"Do not be deceived"** (6:7a). The Galatians' detour into legalism left them drifting through the wasteland of bewilderment, unsure of the implications of accepting a works-centered faith. Paul, however, saw their predicament and exhorted them to get back to the fruitful field of grace. "For whatever a man sows," Paul reasoned, "this he will also reap. For the one who sows to his own flesh shall from the flesh reap corruption, but the one who sows to the Spirit shall from the Spirit reap eternal life" (vv. 7b–8).

III. Weariness in Paul

As we turn to the final two verses in Galatians, we find a tired Paul. He writes as if he has exhausted all his energy in defending the gospel of grace. But before he sends the letter, he squeezes out a few last words.

A. **A request from a weary warrior.** "From now on let no one cause trouble for me" (v. 17a). This does not mean "Don't tell me if you have any more problems with legalism." Paul would certainly want to batter any barrier raised against Christianity (compare 2 Cor. 10:5). Neither is Paul asking the legalists to stop dogging his steps, for he knows they will not. Rather, he is appealing to the Galatian believers to quit troubling him by giving in to legalistic heresies. He wants them to stand strong for the faith, not buckle under to counterfeit gospels.

B. **A reason to be respected.** Why should the Galatian Christians grant Paul's request? Because, Paul says, "I bear on my body the brand-marks of Jesus" (Gal. 6:17b). The scars on Paul's body, which were the result of hardship in Christian service, reveal his relationship to Christ, just as the marks of a branding iron on a first-century slave revealed the owner's identity. Like Christ, Paul bore on his body the genuineness of his faith in God. The Judaizers, however, had only the worthless sign of circumcision to validate their trust in themselves alone.

C. **A benediction.** Paul ends his letter by summarizing the central thrust of the gospel (v. 18). The authentic Christian message begins with God's unmerited favor toward sinners, a favor best exemplified in the death of His Son, the Lord Jesus Christ. And His grace comes to fruition when we abide in it through faith in Christ.

A Final Plea for Freedom

"Paul's arguments have been vigorous. His language, alive in the cause of freedom, has done all that language can do.... No more can be expected of an argument. All that words on parchment can do has been done....

"He now announces that he is done talking about the subject and that he wants us to be done with it too. There is crucifixion to be faced. There is freedom to be lived. There is God to be enjoyed.... Crucifixion puts all other questions, all other concerns, into a subordinate position. Once we face the fact of death [to self] and accept it, there is a sense in which all further religious discussion is parlor talk."[5]

Now is the time to stop *talking* about the free life and start *living* it. If you haven't already done so, open the door of your life to Jesus Christ. Let Him come in and begin circulating the crisp, clean air of spiritual liberty. Then submit yourself daily to the control of His Spirit, allowing His liberating power to permeate everything you feel, think, and do.

 Living Insights

Study One

One of the best cures for forgetfulness is review. After twenty studies in Galatians, let's refresh our memories on the truths we've learned.

- Go back over Galatians and your study notes. As you review each lesson, write down the truths that mean the most to you. (Fill in only the "truth" sections; "application" comes in Study Two.)

GALATIANS: LETTER OF LIBERATION

Set Me Free!

Truth: _____   Application: _____

_____   _____

_____   _____

5. Eugene H. Peterson, *Traveling Light: Reflections on the Free Life* (Downers Grove, Ill.: Inter-Varsity Press, 1982), p. 194.

Another Gospel Is Not *the* Gospel

Truth: _____   Application: _____
_____   _____
_____   _____

A Radical Transformation

Truth: _____   Application: _____
_____   _____
_____   _____

The Value of Acceptance and Affirmation

Truth: _____   Application: _____
_____   _____
_____   _____

Confronting Hypocrisy

Truth: _____   Application: _____
_____   _____
_____   _____

The Exchanged Life

Truth: _____   Application: _____
_____   _____
_____   _____

Backsliding into Legalism

Truth: _____   Application: _____
_____   _____
_____   _____

Delivered from a Curse

Truth: _____   Application: _____
_____   _____
_____   _____

Three Men and a Promise

Truth: _____   Application: _____

_____   _____

_____   _____

Preempting the Paidagogos

Truth: _____   Application: _____

_____   _____

_____   _____

No Longer a Slave—a Son!

Truth: _____   Application: _____

_____   _____

_____   _____

Solving the Pastor-People Conflict

Truth: _____   Application: _____

_____   _____

_____   _____

To Those Who Want to Be under the Law

Truth: _____   Application: _____

_____   _____

_____   _____

Freedom, Faith, Love, and Truth

Truth: _____   Application: _____

_____   _____

_____   _____

Limiting Liberty with Love

Truth: _____   Application: _____

_____   _____

_____   _____

Learning How to Walk

Truth: _____   Application: _____

_____   _____

_____   _____

Gentle Restoration

Truth: _____   Application: _____

_____   _____

_____   _____

The Law of the Harvest

Truth: _____   Application: _____

_____   _____

_____   _____

A Bold, Blunt Reproof

Truth: _____   Application: _____

_____   _____

_____   _____

A Branded Man

Truth: _____   Application: _____

_____   _____

_____   _____

 Living Insights

Study Two ━━━

Now take some time to review how you applied what you've learned. In Study One write down an application for each lesson. Then thank God for helping you to become freer as a result of His message to the Galatians.

Books for Probing Further

It's easy to go along with the crowd, marching to the same tune and beat as everyone else. The Galatian Christians certainly had no trouble falling in line with the pied pipers of legalism. After all, the Judaizers' song had the same lyrics as other songs sung by the world: salvation is achieved, not received. How could the majority be wrong?

Paul knew that all these songs were actually cleverly disguised dirges sung by the spiritually dead to deceive the living. When Paul heard these haunting death chants coming from the lips of the Galatian Christians, he couldn't believe his ears. Why did these Christians change their tune? What could he do to return the lively melody of freedom to their lips? Paul answered the challenge by composing a Spirit-inspired letter pulsating with the driving vitality of liberty in Christ.

We hope you've felt freedom's beat and heard its melody in Paul's letter. Our greatest joy would be to hear that this study has helped you become a member of God's everlasting choir. Of course, once you join a music group, there are new songs to learn and new styles to master. To help you along, we have listed several books that apply the theme of Christian freedom to various areas of life. If, along with consistent Bible study, you read and apply these resources, you will soon hear a richer quality and steadier cadence in your voice. The songs of Christian freedom will begin to flow naturally from you, eventually causing your whole life to resound with the vibrancy of heaven.

I. Liberating Doctrine

Blamires, Harry. *On Christian Truth.* Ann Arbor, Mich.: Servant Books, 1983. "This book," states Blamires in the introduction, "is a mixture of explanation and reflection. It seeks to explain, without jargon but with up-to-date examples, the meaning of some of the central articles of Christian belief. And it reflects on those beliefs in relation to our daily lives—our problems, our worries, and our joys." Like a modern-day C. S. Lewis, Blamires captures the essence of Christianity's liberating truths.

Lightner, Robert P. *Heaven for Those Who Can't Believe.* Foreword by Andrew H. Wood. Schaumburg, Ill.: Regular Baptist Press, 1977. The Galatian epistle deals with salvation on an adult level. It was written to people who had the ability to accept or reject the gospel. But what about those who don't have that ability—babies, young children, or the mentally handicapped? Can people be saved if they can't comprehend? Lightner addresses these questions, using Scripture to defend the position that heaven was also made for those who can't understand the gospel.

II. Challenges to the Free Life

Guinness, Os. *The Gravedigger File.* Downers Grove, Ill.: InterVarsity Press, 1983. Rather than launch an all-out frontal attack, armies will sometimes infiltrate enemy camps to sabotage operations from within. Once their enemies are greatly weakened, the invaders can take over with hardly a shot being fired. In a style reminiscent of C. S. Lewis's *Screwtape Letters,* Guinness alerts us to the presence of clever saboteurs who have already led the Western church to social irrelevance. We're digging our own graves, believes Guinness, but we do have a way out—if we act decisively and soon.

McDowell, Josh, and Don Stewart. *Handbook of Today's Religions.* San Bernardino, Calif.: Here's Life Publishers, 1983. Today the menu of beliefs is cluttered with so many options that we need information to steer us away from those dishes that will upset our biblical stomachs. McDowell and Stewart provide the help we need in this consumer's guide to Christian eating. Concisely and accurately, they expose the ingredients of the major cults, the occult, non-Christian religions, and secular philosophies. This guide is one that none of us should be without.

Morey, Robert A. *The New Atheism and the Erosion of Freedom.* Minneapolis, Minn.: Bethany House Publishers, 1986. Never before has atheism become so popular and militant as it has in the twentieth century. As D. James Kennedy astutely observes in the preface, "With the disastrous success of Communism in the East and the devastating impact of Humanism in the West, atheism has become the religion of the modern unbelieving man." Morey explains how we can recognize atheism's influence and effectively combat it on its own terms. Atheists can become Christians; Morey shows us how.

III. Liberating Others

Aldrich, Joseph C. *Life-style Evangelism.* Foreword by Haddon W. Robinson. Portland, Oreg.: Multnomah Press, 1981. Robinson writes: "Outsiders to faith are first drawn to Christians and then to Christ. Unfortunately, not all Christians attract. Like a turned magnet, some repel. Yet Christians, alive to God, loving, caring, laughing, sharing, involved at the point of people's need, present an undeniable witness for Christ in their society." Aldrich explains how you, too, can attract unbelievers to the Savior in the same way He brought people to Himself.

Pippert, Rebecca Manley. *Out of the Salt Shaker and into the World.* Foreword by Walter Trobisch. Downers Grove, Ill.: InterVarsity

Press, 1979. Pippert begins her book with an astute observation: "Christians and non-Christians have something in common: We're both uptight about evangelism." She's right. Believers are afraid of offending, and unbelievers fear being blasted. The author tackles both problems by showing us how we can relax and help non-Christians lower their defenses as we present the gospel in word and deed.

IV. Living the Free Life

Briscoe, D. Stuart. *Spirit Life.* Old Tappan, N.J.: Fleming H. Revell Co., 1983. From our study in Galatians, we now know we should bear the fruit of the Spirit. But we need to turn our knowledge into action. How can we cultivate and grow love, joy, peace, patience, kindness, goodness, faithfulness, meekness, and self-control? We can't on our own, but we can when we yield to the Spirit. Briscoe points the way to the Spirit-filled life we all are meant to enjoy.

Sittser, Jerry. *The Adventure: Putting Energy into Your Walk with God.* Foreword by Leighton Ford. Downers Grove, Ill.: InterVarsity Press, 1985. "I want to motivate Christians to be mature disciples," writes Sittser in the preface. "I believe that there is drama in the Christian life. It is full of wonder and power. By its very nature it will not allow us to be casual in the way we live it out. The Christian life demands commitment and promises adventure. I want readers to catch the vision. I want them to gain a sense of destiny." Do yourself a favor. Join Sittser in his fresh, exciting approach to the Christian life.

Acknowledgments

Insight for Living is grateful for permission to quote from the following sources:

Boice, James Montgomery. "Galatians." Taken from *The Expositor's Bible Commentary,* by Frank E. Gaebelein. Copyright 1976 by The Zondervan Corporation.

Goodrum, Randy. "You Needed Me." Copyright 1975 by Chappell and Company and Ironside Music. All rights administered by Chappell and Company. International copyright secured. All rights reserved.

Peterson, Eugene H. *Traveling Light: Reflections on the Free Life.* Downers Grove, Ill.: InterVarsity Press, 1982.

Stott, John R. W. *The Message of Galatians: Only One Way.* The Bible Speaks Today Series. Downers Grove, Ill.: InterVarsity Press, 1982.

Notes

Notes

Notes

Notes

Notes

Insight for Living
Cassette Tapes
GALATIANS

Freedom is such a glorious gift! Ask anyone who has been released from prison or has escaped from a nation that oppresses its people. But the chains that hold us in bondage are not always visible. Demonic influence can imprison as easily as steel bars. And the subtle grip of legalism can hold Christians captive as surely as shackles. This slavery to the Law's demands is no stranger to the Church. Paul's letter to the Galatians, though, proclaims that today, as then, we have a liberator. By His grace alone Christ can break the chains of the "gospel" of works and set us free.

			U.S.	Canadian
GAL	CS	Cassette series—includes album cover	$55.25	$70.00
		Individual cassettes—include messages		
		A and B	5.00	6.35

These prices are effective as of July 1987 and are subject to change without notice.

GAL 1-A: *Set Me Free!*—Survey of Galatians
　　 B: *Another Gospel Is Not the Gospel*—Galatians 1:1–10

GAL 2-A: *A Radical Transformation*—Galatians 1:11–24
　　 B: *The Value of Acceptance and Affirmation*—Galatians 2:1–10

GAL 3-A: *Confronting Hypocrisy*—Galatians 2:11–16, Acts 14:24–15:11
　　 B: *The Exchanged Life*—Galatians 2:17–21, Isaiah 40:28–31

GAL 4-A: *Backsliding into Legalism*—Galatians 3:1–9
　　 B: *Delivered from a Curse*—Galatians 3:10–14

GAL 5-A: *Three Men and a Promise*—Galatians 3:15–22
　　 B: *Preempting the Paidagogos*—Galatians 3:23–29

GAL 6-A: *No Longer a Slave—a Son!*—Galatians 4:1–11
　　 B: *Solving the Pastor-People Conflict*—Galatians 4:12–20

GAL 7-A: *To Those Who Want to Be under the Law*—Galatians 4:21–31
　　 B: *Freedom, Faith, Love, and Truth*—Galatians 5:1–12

GAL 8-A: *Limiting Liberty with Love*—Galatians 5:13–15, Romans 14:13–23
　　 B: *Learning How to Walk*—Galatians 5:16–25

GAL 9-A: *Gentle Restoration*—Galatians 5:26–6:5
　　 B: *The Law of the Harvest*—Galatians 6:6–10

GAL 10-A: *A Bold, Blunt Reproof*—Galatians 6:11–16
　　 B: *A Branded Man*—Galatians 6:17–18, 2 Corinthians 11:23–28

Ordering Information

U.S. ordering information: You are welcome to use our toll-free number (for Visa and MasterCard orders only) between the hours of 8:30 A.M. and 4:00 P.M., Pacific time, Monday through Friday. The number is **(800) 772-8888.** This number may be used anywhere in the continental United States except California, Hawaii, and Alaska. Orders from these areas are handled through our Sales Department at **(714) 870-9161.** We are unable to accept collect calls.

Your order will be processed promptly. We ask that you allow four to six weeks for delivery by fourth-class mail. If you wish your order to be shipped first-class, please add 10 percent of the total order cost (not including California sales tax) for shipping and handling.

Canadian ordering information: Your order will be processed promptly. We ask that you allow approximately four weeks for delivery. All orders will be shipped from our Canadian office. For our listeners in British Columbia, a 6 percent sales tax must be added to the total of all tape orders (not including postage). For further information, please contact our office at **(604) 272-5811.**

Payment options: We accept personal checks, money orders, Visa, and MasterCard in payment for materials ordered. Unfortunately, we are unable to offer invoicing or COD orders. If the amount of your check or money order is less than the amount of your purchase, your check will be returned so that you may place your order again with the correct amount. All orders must be paid in full before shipment can be made.

Returned checks: There is a $10 charge for any returned check (regardless of the amount of your order) to cover processing and invoicing.

Guarantee: Our tapes are guaranteed for ninety days against faulty performance or breakage due to a defect in the tape. For best results, please be sure your tape recorder is in good operating condition and is cleaned regularly.

Mail your order to one of the following addresses:

Insight for Living
Sales Department
Post Office Box 4444
Fullerton, CA 92634

Insight for Living Ministries
Post Office Box 2510
Vancouver, BC
Canada V6B 3W7

Quantity discounts and gift certificates are available upon request.

Overseas Ordering Information

If you do not live in the United States or Canada, please note the following information. This will ensure efficient processing of your request.

Estimated time of delivery: We ask that you allow approximately twelve to sixteen weeks for delivery by surface mail. If you would like your order sent airmail, the length of delivery may be reduced. All orders will be shipped from our office in Fullerton, California.

Payment options: Due to fluctuating currency rates, we can accept only personal checks made payable in U.S. funds, international money orders, Visa, and MasterCard in payment for materials ordered. If the amount of your check or money order is less than the amount of your purchase, your check will be returned so that you may place your order again with the correct amount. All orders must be paid in full before shipment can be made.

Returned checks: There is a $10 charge for any returned check (regardless of the amount of your order) to cover processing and invoicing.

Postage and handling: Please add to the amount of purchase the postage cost for the service you desire. All orders must include postage based on the chart below.

Purchase Amount		Surface Postage	Airmail Postage
From	To	Percentage of Order	Percentage of Order
$ .01	$15.00	40%	75%
15.01	75.00	25%	45%
75.01	or more	15%	40%

Guarantee: Our tapes are guaranteed for ninety days against faulty performance or breakage due to a defect in the tape. For best results, please be sure your tape recorder is in good operating condition and is cleaned regularly.

Mail your order or inquiry to the following address:

Insight for Living
Sales Department
Post Office Box 4444
Fullerton, CA 92634

Quantity discounts and gift certificates are available upon request.

Order Form

Please send me the following cassette tapes:

The current series: ☐ GAL CS Galatians: Letter of Liberation

Individual cassettes: ☐ GAL 1 ☐ GAL 2 ☐ GAL 3 ☐ GAL 4
☐ GAL 5 ☐ GAL 6 ☐ GAL 7 ☐ GAL 8
☐ GAL 9 ☐ GAL 10

I am enclosing:

$_____ To purchase the cassette series for $55.25 (in Canada $70.00*) which includes the album cover

$_____ To purchase individual tapes at $5.00 each (in Canada $6.35*)

$_____ Total of purchases

$_____ If the order will be delivered in California, please add 6 percent sales tax

$_____ U.S. residents please add 10 percent for first-class shipping and handling if desired

$_____ *British Columbia residents please add 6 percent sales tax

$_____ Canadian residents please add 6 percent for postage

$_____ **Overseas residents please add appropriate postage** (See postage chart under "Overseas Ordering Information.")

$_____ As a gift to the Insight for Living radio ministry for which a tax-deductible receipt will be issued

$_____ **Total amount due (Please do not send cash.)**

Form of payment:

☐ Check or money order made payable to Insight for Living

☐ Credit card (Visa or MasterCard only)

If there is a balance: ☐ apply it as a donation ☐ please refund

---

Credit card purchases:

☐ Visa ☐ MasterCard number _____

Expiration date _____

Signature _____

We cannot process your credit card purchase without your signature.

Name _____

Address _____

_____

City _____

State/Province _____ Zip/Postal code _____

Country _____

Telephone ( ) _____ Radio station __ __ __ __

Should questions arise concerning your order, we may need to contact you.

Order Form

Please send me the following cassette tapes:

The current series: ☐ GAL CS Galatians: Letter of Liberation

Individual cassettes: ☐ GAL 1 ☐ GAL 2 ☐ GAL 3 ☐ GAL 4

☐ GAL 5 ☐ GAL 6 ☐ GAL 7 ☐ GAL 8

☐ GAL 9 ☐ GAL 10

I am enclosing:

$ _____ To purchase the cassette series for $55.25 (in Canada $70.00*) which includes the album cover

$ _____ To purchase individual tapes at $5.00 each (in Canada $6.35*)

$ _____ Total of purchases

$ _____ If the order will be delivered in California, please add 6 percent sales tax

$ _____ U.S. residents please add 10 percent for first-class shipping and handling if desired

$ _____ *British Columbia residents please add 6 percent sales tax

$ _____ Canadian residents please add 6 percent for postage

$ _____ **Overseas residents please add appropriate postage** (See postage chart under "Overseas Ordering Information.")

$ _____ As a gift to the Insight for Living radio ministry for which a tax-deductible receipt will be issued

$ _____ **Total amount due (Please do not send cash.)**

Form of payment:

☐ Check or money order made payable to Insight for Living

☐ Credit card (Visa or MasterCard only)

If there is a balance: ☐ apply it as a donation ☐ please refund

---

Credit card purchases:

☐ Visa ☐ MasterCard number _____

Expiration date _____

Signature _____

We cannot process your credit card purchase without your signature.

Name _____

Address _____

_____

City _____

State/Province _____ Zip/Postal code _____

Country _____

Telephone (___) _____ Radio station ___ ___ ___ ___

Should questions arise concerning your order, we may need to contact you.

Order Form

Please send me the following cassette tapes:

The current series: ☐ GAL CS Galatians: Letter of Liberation

Individual cassettes: ☐ GAL 1 ☐ GAL 2 ☐ GAL 3 ☐ GAL 4
☐ GAL 5 ☐ GAL 6 ☐ GAL 7 ☐ GAL 8
☐ GAL 9 ☐ GAL 10

I am enclosing:

$ _____ To purchase the cassette series for $55.25 (in Canada $70.00*) which includes the album cover

$ _____ To purchase individual tapes at $5.00 each (in Canada $6.35*)

$ _____ Total of purchases

$ _____ If the order will be delivered in California, please add 6 percent sales tax

$ _____ U.S. residents please add 10 percent for first-class shipping and handling if desired

$ _____ *British Columbia residents please add 6 percent sales tax

$ _____ Canadian residents please add 6 percent for postage

$ _____ **Overseas residents please add appropriate postage** (See postage chart under "Overseas Ordering Information.")

$ _____ As a gift to the Insight for Living radio ministry for which a tax-deductible receipt will be issued

$ _____ **Total amount due (Please do not send cash.)**

Form of payment:

☐ Check or money order made payable to Insight for Living
☐ Credit card (Visa or MasterCard only)
If there is a balance: ☐ apply it as a donation ☐ please refund

Credit card purchases:
☐ Visa ☐ MasterCard number _____
Expiration date _____
Signature _____
We cannot process your credit card purchase without your signature.

Name _____
Address _____
_____
City _____
State/Province _____ Zip/Postal code _____
Country _____
Telephone ( ) _____ Radio station __ __ __ __
Should questions arise concerning your order, we may need to contact you.